INVENTING CANADA

My dearest Father-in-law,

Perhaps we "colonials" are
due a bit more credit
after all !!

Have a wonderful and happy
Christmas!

All my love and best wishes,

INVENTING CANADA

100 Years of Innovation

ROY MAYER

RAINCOAST BOOKS

Vancouver

First published in 1997 by

Raincoast Books
8680 Cambie Street
Vancouver, B.C.
V6P 6M9
(604) 323-7100

1 2 3 4 5 6 7 8 9 10

CANADIAN CATALOGUING IN PUBLICATION DATA

Mayer, Roy.
Inventing Canada

ISBN 1-55192-113-8

1. Inventors – Canada – Biography. 2. Inventions – Canada – History. I. Title.

T39.M39 1997   609.2'271   C97-910456-4

Grateful acknowledgement is made to the Hants Journal
*for permission to reprint "Rubber Reptile Ruptured in
Dill Pumpkin Patch" in Chapter 9. Reprinted
by permission of Glen Parker.*

Printed in Canada

To my wonderful and imaginative family:

my loving wife Lise, daughter Elizabeth,

and son Tedd, with gratitude

for always being there

Contents

Acknowledgements

At the outset I extend sincere thanks to Eric Ranger and Denny Shortliffe for being able to count on their valuable assistance and knowledge of computer programming, and to Michael Carroll, formerly the managing editor at Raincoast Books, for his much-appreciated assistance.

The primary research for this book was based upon a considerable amount of material provided from files available at the Canadian Intellectual Properties Office (CIPO) of Industry Canada. CIPO personnel – including Monik Burchinshaw, Diane Lafontaine, Richard Lebel, and especially Richard MacDonald of the Patent Search Room – were most helpful and provided a professional service far beyond what I could have expected.

At the National Research Council, Dick Doyle was a superb source of inspiration and of information about Canadian innovators, as the secretary to the selection committee of the Canadian Science and Engineering Hall of Fame, which is now under the custodianship of the National Museum of Science and Technology. Lynn Delgaty of NRC Photo Archives lent a valuable hand on several occasions, even on her own time.

Marion Grobb in the Communications Branch at the National Museum of Science and Technology, and Sylvie Bertrand in Resources, have been a great help.

In addition, many people from various walks of life cheerfully and expeditiously helped me to gather excellent information for each of the stories of our outstanding innovators. I will draw special attention to each of these people for their much-appreciated assistance.

In chapter I, on JAMES GOSLING, Dr. Michael Cowpland; and Robin Coran, Sun Microsystems JAVA Incorporated, Los Angeles; and on MIKE POTTER, Alan Rottenberg and Silvana Crea, Cognos

Incorporated; on Dr. Michael Cowpland, James Bagnall, *Ottawa Citizen*; and Michelle Murphy-Croteau, Corel Corporation.

In chapter 2, on Dr. Tofy Mussivand, Gene Shershen, president, Ottawa Inventors Association; Special Assistant Lisa Fabricius, University of Ottawa Heart Institute; and Michelle Wyndham-West, the World Heart Corporation, Ottawa; on Dr. John A. Hopps, Don Hopps; Dick Doyle, National Research Council, Ottawa; and *Passing Pulses,* by John A. Hopps, published by CMBES Secretariat (1995).

In chapter 3, on Dr. James Naismith, Terry Craig, director, and John Gosset, special advisor, Dr. James Naismith Centre, Almonte, Ontario; Bonnie Naismith McBain; Margaret Miller, director, Basketball Canada; *The Basketball Man James Naismith,* by Bernice Larson Webb, published by University of Kansas Press (1973); and the video *The Father of Basketball,* by Leaps and Bounds Incorporated; on The Birthplace of Hockey, Roy MacGregor, *Ottawa Citizen* journalist and author; *The Puck Starts Here,* by Garth Vaughan, distributed by General Distribution (1996); and on Tom Pashby, Roy MacGregor, *Ottawa Citizen* journalist and author; Murray Costello, Canadian Hockey Association; and Peter Stephenson, vice president, technical, Badminton Canada.

In chapter 4, on Michael Germain, "The Bay" perfume counter salespeople; on Thor Grundell, Rick Chapell, the Pacific Salmon Foundation; Sandra Cachez, Pacific Salmon Gift Store, Capilano Canyon Fish Hatchery, North Vancouver; Vicky Davis, librarian, the Canadian Conservation Institute, Ottawa; and *Innerskins/Outerskins: Gut and Fishskin,* by Pat Hickman, published by San Francisco Craft and Folk Art Museum (1987).

In chapter 5, on Joseph-Armand Bombardier, France Bissonnette, president, Céline Chauvette, director, and Karl Eisen, curator, Bombardier Museum; and *Joseph-Armand Bombardier, an Inventor's Dream Come True,* by Roger Lacasse, published by Libre Expression (1988); on J.G. Wright, Industry Canada Information Directorate; on Thomas Ahearn, great-granddaughter and family historian Lilias Ahearn; Catherine Ahearn; Glen Beaton, Ahearn & Soper, Electrical Engineers; and Dave Bullock, assistant archivist, City of Ottawa Archives.

In chapter 6, on Reginald A. Fessenden, Dr. Jack Belrose,

director of radio, Communications Research Centre; John Fessenden, Waterloo; Bob Fessenden, Edmonton; Knowlton Museum, Knowlton, Quebec; and *Reginald Fessenden, Radio's Forgotten Voice,* by Michael Webb, published by Copp Clark Pitman (1991); on KENNETH O. HILL, Marilyn Golding, Ernest C. Manning Awards Foundation, Calgary; Kevin Shackell, Communications Research Centre; and on TIM COLLINGS, Marilyn Golding, Ernest C. Manning Awards Foundation, Calgary.

In chapter 7, on CANADA'S INNOVATION CENTRE, Linda Hendry, manager, Carol Stewart, publications manager, and Carolyn Parks, marketing assistant, Innovation Centre.

In chapter 8, on JIM BEAUDOIN, Tom Spears, *Ottawa Citizen* science writer; on AVI FRIEDMAN, Ron Andrews and Deborah Lodoen, Canada Mortgage and Housing Corporation.

In chapter 9, on DRS. BURTON CRAIG AND KEITH DOWNEY, Dick Doyle, National Research Council, Ottawa; *From Rapeseed to Canola, the Billion Dollar Success Story,* by Katherine Lawrence, published by the National Research Council (1992); and *One Hundred Harvests,* by Research Branch, Agriculture Canada (1886-1986); on DR. MAURICE MOLONEY, Richard Starnes, *Ottawa Citizen*; and Andrea Berg, University of Calgary; and on HOWARD DILL, Roy MacGregor, *Ottawa Citizen* journalist and author; and *The Pumpkin King,* by Al Kingsbury, published by Lancelot Press (1996).

In chapter 10, on PAUL TOYNE, Richard Albert, Canada Games Company; on CHRIS HANEY AND SCOTT ABBOTT, Jim Ware, president, Horn Abbot Limited; and CBC made-for-TV movie *Breaking All the Rules.*

In chapter 11, on HUGH LE CAINE, Dick Doyle, National Research Council, Ottawa; Mrs. Trudi Le Caine; and *The Sackbutt Blues,* by Gayle Young, published by the National Museum of Science and Technology (1989); and on NESTOR BURTNYK, Dick Doyle, National Research Council, Ottawa.

To all of the innovators I have interviewed for this book, I offer my profound thanks for your assistance, together with my gratitude for putting zing into my life with your creative contributions to the world.

INTRODUCTION
The Canadian Heroes

This book is about truly inspired Canadians from various walks of life who committed themselves to originating something new and necessary, took up the creative challenge, and followed it through to success. Such a journey is fraught with risk and is a fierce challenge to necessary personal attributes, not the least of which are nerves of steel and a relentless determination to follow through, whatever the consequences.

Even though every manufactured thing around us was first created by an innovator, and even some of nature's creations have been replaced or enhanced by an invention, the common view of this process is very narrow. One purpose of this book is to show that some important innovations are not within the purview of proprietary rights conferred by the patent office upon an innovator. In addition, some things are not patentable but are nonetheless significant inventions, as a few of the accounts in this book reveal.

The subjects offered here include both historical and contemporary innovators whose contributions impact upon the quality of our lives today. For each of the biographical sketches, I have personally interviewed either the innovators themselves or their living descendants and friends, gleaned information from news media reports, books, biographies, and family scrapbooks, and sought advice from authorities in the respective fields in order to present accurate and entertaining chronicles of these extraordinary people and their innovations.

Readers may be surprised to discover some important facts that they were previously unaware of concerning our Canadian innovators. Their relatively low profiles may have something to do with our reputation for not wanting to blow our own horn, to be properly modest. I understand this, yet I am proud of the innovative and legendary genius that Canadians contribute to the world and am grateful for this opportunity to show off some of their great achievements.

The chapters in this book are representative of a wide cross-section of endeavour. In each piece I have tried to be especially sensitive to personal insights so that the reader can appreciate the human dimensions of each story and enjoy identifying with each situation.

Our innovators have given novelty, variety, and colour to our lives with their great practical gifts, and the world would be an exceedingly boring and grey place without their vitality. I hope that this book will foster a greater understanding and appreciation of these imaginative and productive people who have taken breathtaking chances with the success of their careers and have often suffered financial failure and a fall from social grace for their efforts unless or until they have made a lot of money and have been successful in the eyes of their peers.

I

High-Tech
Power Players

Java Jolts the Hi-Tech Highways

James Gosling

When I spoke to James Gosling, the inventor of Java, that sensational general-purpose computer-programming language and the common language of the Internet, he casually took his brilliant mind with a grain of salt and tossed it off in favour of hard work: "Inspiration isn't ninety-nine percent," he said, "it's only one percent, and the rest, the ninety-nine percent part, is perspiration. If anything, I've learned that...." James knows this full well because, even though he is one of those rare people who can solve a problem so intricate that most of us can't even understand the predicament itself, he has spent a number of years on innovative developments only to be squelched most of the time by a lack of internal support. He has seen products inferior to his become successes due to the backing of powerful marketing promotion. He has been stifled by what he calls "antibodies": co-workers so focused on their own outlook that they suppress any new concepts. But James is a patient man by nature and has ultimate faith in himself and in working hard to bring about a successful conclusion. And it works!

James's internationality as an inventor follows a path that intrigues me. In my research on inventors and their inventions, the common thread among innovative people, even going back to the 1800s when travel was very time consuming and expensive, has been their constant touring and summering or wintering in different countries. Raising his

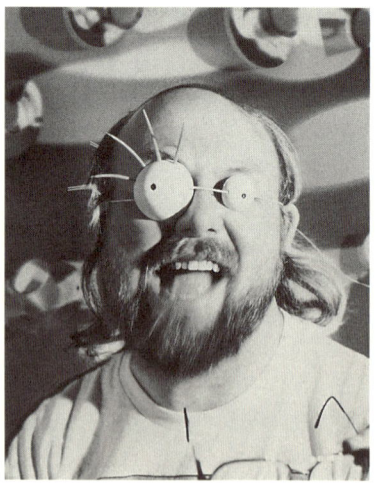

Computer programming genius Dr. James Gosling.

family in California, visiting close relatives fairly frequently in Alberta, and taking business trips to Japan or elsewhere several times each year give James a membership in the same club as other leading inventors, such as Alexander Graham Bell, who had close relatives in Scotland, worked in Canada when he invented the telephone, and summered here in later years when he invented many other items (including aircraft) and then wintered in the United States; Guglielmo Marconi, an Italian citizen at the time that he demonstrated the first so-called transoceanic transmission of a telegraphic signal while working in Canada and Great Britain; Reginald Fessenden, the Canadian inventor of radio, television, sonar, and hundreds of other exceptional items, who worked out of the United States for many years but also resided in Bermuda; Sir Sandford Fleming, another diverse inventor, who came up with the standard time system while he lived and worked almost simultaneously in England, Canada, and the United States; and Michael Cowpland, originally from England, who became a Canadian citizen and works between Ottawa, Dublin, and Salt Lake City and travels around the world constantly. Since these extraordinary people are in such demand and are so mobile by virtue of their calling, it is impossible today to offhandedly identify their citizenship.

The citizenship of some world-renowned inventors many years ago is still strongly debated today, and the confusion is understandable. However, there is no confusion about James Gosling's proud identity as a Canadian, although I expect that Gosling will spend much of his life in many other countries around the world.

James Gosling was born on May 19, 1955, on a farm near Calgary, where he lived with his older sister Barb and his younger brother Geoff. His mother, Joyce, was a teacher, and his father David worked in oil exploration throughout the North.

"When I was a kid, I was always interested in building 'stuff' that didn't cost me anything," James recalls. At 12 he made an electronic tic-tac-toe game with parts from a telephone switch and a TV set that he found while sifting through his grandfather's used-equipment junkyard. It was at the age of 14 that he discovered what would become his destiny, computers, when friends of his parents introduced him to the computer mainframe at the University of Calgary, located just up the road from his home. He memorized the numbers on the combination door lock pads, so he was able to let himself into the university whenever he wanted to create "stuff." Looking back on this pastime today, he jokingly calls this his "B and E" type of education; he would simply let himself in, work on the computer in the physics class where he got to know some people, and leave whenever he felt like it. Apparently everyone became accustomed to his being there, and he suspected that the profs who noticed him thought that some authority had invited him there, and they weren't about to challenge him because he seemed to know what he was doing. James certainly did know, and 18 months later he was hired by the university to write software for the ISIS-II satellite project. On reflection he is proud that, while some kids did drugs, he did software. After skipping what he feels were a "reasonable" number of classes, James graduated from high school, earned his bachelor of science degree from the University of Calgary, and then received his doctorate from Carnegie-Mellon University in Pittsburgh.

Gosling's first job was writing software at International Business Machines (IBM), but the company didn't seem to regard his work seriously since it never produced any of it, making James feel uncomfortable. "I felt like an idiot for working there. They looked at me like I was a large wild animal that had taken a bullet to the head and was just taking a while to die," he says.

In the meantime James considered an offer from Sun Microsystems. Finally, in 1984, he joined Sun, setting the stage for his invention of Java some 12 years later. His initial assignment was to provide Sun workstations with a new screen appearance, or user interface, designed to make computers easier to operate.

During this period he began to channel his efforts toward refining an idea for a universal programming language for small electronic devices. The basic premise was that the tiny, inexpensive computer controls being built into everything from cars to microwave ovens are powered by imbedded microprocessors, and since he recognized that there was no uniform, interconnecting software language in this imbedded world, he would invent one to enable all of these electronic digital devices to share information and to speak to one another. He envisioned a programming language that would run on the microprocessor for any device and establish communication between them. This could be the vast, untapped market James was seeking. The year was 1991.

"This vision kept evolving," says James. "The basic idea was to try to build interfaces that people could actually use on simple devices. The Mac user interface is great, but it's a desktop system, and only a small fraction of the universe is on desks. So the idea was to come up with the user interface for the rest of the universe. There just wasn't any language that could do the job, so I had to write one. I had to call it something, so I named it for the tree that was growing outside my window."

At the time James didn't know that the software he dubbed Oak would later be renamed Java. Because computer software until then had only been compatible with the microprocessor on which it was written, he decided to create a virtual machine inside his Oak program to enable the software to run on any operating system. James kept up with this period of industry evolvement and suffered through a mounting number of disappointments, countered by glimmers of encouraging market indicators from time to time.

By 1994 the hi-tech highway had swung toward low-bandwidth on-line networks, the precursor of the World Wide Web opening the door to reach potential consumers en masse, and James realized that this was finally the perfect vehicle for his new electronic dialect. The Web was the ideal environment for Oak technology. As a network the Web consisted of literally millions of electronic devices with assorted microprocessors, all connected and communicating together. Sun Microsystems then prepared to plug James's software invention into the white-hot trend of the industry. The core of the plan was that the software could be utilized inside an Internet "browser" program. At that point the Web exploded into a star. James and his team decided that a dynamic image for his creation was crucial, so they sat around a bucketful of M & Ms and brainstormed until the name Java burst into being.

In two years Java, James Gosling's universal computer software language, handily overtook the world stage, with orders for 30 million Java-capable machines to be manufactured in the first year alone.

For the future Gosling looks to Java's potential in areas other than the Internet, such as linking up business computers with surrounding office equipment, suppliers, and outside service contractors. Java also works well with home computers in linking up with the tiny computer brains in cars, stoves, microwave ovens, home entertainment equipment, and house alarm systems, to take the smart house a step further.

Dr. James Gosling, his wife Judy, and their daughter Kate live in Redwood City, California, but if history is any indicator, in the future we can expect James and his family to be living anywhere else in the world where he can pursue other great innovative challenges.

COGNOS:
WHERE BUSINESS INTELLIGENCE
WAS BORN

Mike Potter

Mike Potter and I settled down one cool and rainy Sunday morning in early spring to lounge comfortably with a morning coffee before a gently crackling fire in the den, surrounded by floor-to-ceiling glass that gave a sense of being outside with the birds and squirrels that busily picked at the ground for food, at the edge of the melting snow and under the lush evergreens. I was surprised when this exceptional man of imagination explained how he had participated in the design of this large estate and residence. Having a fair knowledge of the complexities one must deal with in this type of construction with its antique stone restoration, extensive glazing, and the choice of finishes and treatments for a residence of this size, I looked around at the innovative design and realized that only a man of his calibre could even entertain pulling off such an achievement. So I just sat back, relaxed, and enjoyed listening to his exceptional career adventure unfold.

In 1944 a baby born to Alan and Joan Potter in London, England, while World War II raged through Europe, was destined to become a dynamic force in the high-technology industry in Canada and around the world some 40 years later. He joined his brother Geoff, who is one year older. Mike characterizes the Potter family as coming "up from the ranks," and they had to be hard working and resourceful to survive in those days of the 1940s and 1950s, when there wasn't any kind of social safety net for those who struggled to cope with raising a family on a low income.

Things started to look up for the Potters when they arrived in Canada in 1951 and the little Potters' grades from elementary school were transferred from London and Newcastle, England, to Vancouver, Winnipeg, Victoria, and eventually Hamilton. Their father was a vacuum cleaner salesman who sought and followed opportunities wherever they were. It was tough on young Mike, but he says that these continual exercises in determination must have affected his own outlook. Finally the Potters settled down somewhat, and in 1958 Mike entered high school in Victoria, where they came to rest. While living in this beautiful seaport, young Mike displayed a keen interest in joining the navy and becoming a ship's captain some day, an aspiration that suited his fascination for things scientific.

When Mike graduated from high school in 1961, he opted for military training, enrolling at Collège Militaire Royale in St. Jean, Quebec. In 1966 he graduated from Royal Military College in Kingston with a bachelor of mathematics degree, and in 1967 he received a masters of physics degree from the University of British Columbia. By this time Mike had concluded that, although he enjoyed military service, he didn't intend to spend a lifetime in it, so he managed to get a posting to the Defence Research Board in Ottawa doing a job in the field of "operations research" that perfectly suited his academic qualifications. After working there for three years as a serviceman in the Armed Forces, Mike shifted to a similar job in the federal government until 1972, modelling the transportation of grain through various ports.

By this time Mike had garnered solid academic credentials, absorbed disciplinary character from Armed Forces duty, and applied his knowledge of mathematics to address some interesting problems in

Mike Potter invented Cognos, where business intelligence was born.

the transportation of one of the nation's major resources. Now he was all set to take on the world.

The year 1972 would prove to be the turning point in Mike Potter's life. Opportunity in the form of computer program outsourcing was knocking hard on Mike's door. To some extent computer consulting firms were employment agencies, and were sometimes referred to as "body shops" in those days, because there was a limited number of computer specialists who applied to these computer service firms who were called on to bid for the rather large contracts, and often these specialists simply went with one or more of the most popular bidders who offered the highest pay. Working on contract was a good way for a computer consulting firm to keep overhead expenses down while being available to handle these contracts, which tended to be short- or medium-term contracts to satisfy the client's immediate needs to plan, install, maintain, or change the management of an information system. It was also profitable for the specialists, who often enjoyed the excitement of working in spurts for a lot of money. Because computers were then so novel and very expensive for an organization to start up, even though the expense was necessary in order to be competitive and efficient, it was much easier for clients to ease their way into the fray, contract by contract, by outsourcing with firms such as Mike's Quasar Systems.

On the downside at the time was the difficulty in obtaining venture capital for players in this new and brash labour-intensive side of the industry. Financiers realized that these firms only had the intrinsic value of their workers on assignment, because it appeared that, without the computer specialists to farm out to an assignment, there was nothing left. Otherwise, capital assets were negligible except for receivables. So, even when firms such as Quasar Systems were able to obtain "requests to tender" from potential clients on the basis of their innovative recommendations, then successfully attract, hire, and organize the specialists, and finally win and fulfill a contract, the extensive financing of high wages for these computer specialists was not readily available from outside financing institutions. And greater numbers of "bodies" out on contract meant greater financing needs, to the extent that financing strains grew with success. But with discipline and innovative leadership, Mike's company was able to finance itself and progressively build Quasar Systems into a multi-million-dollar business by the end of the 1970s.

"From day one at Quasar Systems, our stock-in-trade was innovative computer programming – that's what made us a blue-chip service firm," says Mike. "But the trend toward computer consulting finally softened, and in response we went through a major transition. Bob Minns, our nuts-and-bolts computer scientist, spearheaded a development team, the 'intellectual soul and creative impact of the company,' to eventually create the highly successful advanced programming language called PowerHouse. Since then we've sold over one billion dollars' worth of PowerHouse and, even seventeen years later, continue at the rate of seventy-five million dollars to ninety million dollars per year."

Under Mike Potter, this development team held the lamp that led the way to fundamental change from providing computer services to build software applications to selling tools so that clients could build and customize their own. "We decided that, instead of standardizing applications of the type we were building for our clients, why not make tools for companies to use in building their own systems, with all the exact features they would want," he says. Along with the radical new business focus, Mike decided to establish a new corporate image to describe the kind of people in the new company and its business outlook. He appropriately named the new firm Cognos, which in Latin means "to have knowledge."

Mike found that, to be most effective, innovation needed to originate at the grassroots level rather than from the corporate boardroom on down. This key element of the environment at Cognos largely accounts for why the company is known internally as being one that listens to its people.

Starting in the mid-1980s, PCs became increasingly more popular business equipment, but initially they were only used at each workstation for self-contained operations such as word processing, spreadsheets, and sometimes small accounting systems. Toward the end of the 1980s, PCs began to connect to each other with windows graphics to be part of the "client-server" platform on which serious business applications would be built. But PowerHouse was designed for midrange multiuser systems as opposed to the client-server world, so the end of the PowerHouse cycle was in sight.

Enter Alan Rottenberg in 1989. Born in 1949 in Montreal, a B.A. grad from McGill University in 1972, with a solid sales background that extended to computer sales in 1976, he was vice president of sales for Simware Incorporated just before joining Mike Potter at Cognos. The Cognos team, which included Bob Minns, Jim Sinclair, Robin McNeill, and Don Leonardo, started work on a new client-server "business-intelligence" product in 1987. When Alan came on the scene, he recognized the business-intelligence genius that lurked within the program, and in early 1990 he released the technology under the new brand name of PowerPlay.

Early success was elusive, so Alan advised, "Like a young boxer, if we take care not to overmatch him too soon, PowerPlay can become a champion." So he reevaluated PowerPlay and reintroduced the product, which soon started showing the success that would make it the centrepiece of Cognos's highly successful business-intelligence tools.

Then in 1990 Procter & Gamble, which had already been involved in PowerPlay, was approached to partner on a new reporting capability that would come to be known as Impromptu. This software had been in research and development for several years. Alan explains the creative feat: "Writing a software program that works is one thing, but writing one that has all the possible combinations built-in to culminate in a thoroughly comprehensive program is extremely difficult and complex."

Under the innovative leadership of Alan, with support from Mike, the near impossible became reality. The emergence of these dynamic new products renewed Cognos, and the revenue they attracted grew to $160 million within five years, making Cognos the world leader in business-intelligence software.

While in 1980 PowerHouse gave computers the ability to perform considerably faster, in 1990 PowerPlay and Impromptu enabled computers to be used to support decision making by immediately accessing business intelligence for the user, who no longer had to rely totally on intuition. PowerPlay enabled users to ask questions and develop information in quick sequence, prompting new outlooks and views. Based on the data, a question would be posed and answered, prompting another to be asked and answered, and so on. In the space of five minutes, 12 questions might be presented, the information for each digested, and decisions reached all with the elimination of massive computer printout reports and evaluation and the loss of business opportunity to the user because of the time-consuming nature of the old process. The impact upon the efficient use of computers in business around the world provided by Cognos has been, and continues to be, an enormous contribution to the welfare of industry and government.

Mike has devoted much of his life to his role in business, so when he retired from Cognos Incorporated in September 1995, at only 51 years of age, many people were surprised. He had decided that there is a fabulously interesting world beyond computers and business to explore, so he left Cognos to see what he'd been missing. Along with his wife Alana and their infant daughter Michaela, Mike plans to sail around the world in a few years in a 92-foot, two-masted ketch that he is having built in Holland. This round-the-world trip will be the first for Michaela, although Mike, and more recently Alana, have many deep-water-cruising miles behind them in their current boat. Meanwhile, the three adventurers enjoy the spirit of freedom together, often flying in his multiengine aircraft to explore exciting new destinations.

COMMUNICATIONS LUMINARY

Michael Cowpland

Although the hi-tech industry is usually considered a modern phenomenon, it actually began in 1876 when the telephone was invented by celebrated Canadian innovator Dr. Alexander Graham Bell. When I interviewed today's celebrated Canadian innovator, Dr. Michael Cowpland, I was startled to discover that the fabulous age of telecommunications actually sprang to life, after many years of stagnation, under his innovative leadership. During our discussions, his passion for telecommunications and high technology came through vividly and, even though they're a century apart, the lives of these two great scientists are parallel in so many ways that it seems only natural that he had picked up where Bell had left off when he died in 1922. Before Cowpland came along, it seemed as though telephones were never expected to evolve much beyond basic uses despite being the sole thoroughfare of instant communications throughout the world. There were

When Dr. Michael Cowpland speaks, the world listens.

exhaustive discussions about the wired-city concept and how it could work, but Cowpland was already well along with a futuristic plan that was destined to rapidly permeate the world as nothing had before. It was finally here – the wired world that Bell had glimpsed and started in motion in the 1870s was to become a reality 100 years later due to the inventive genius of Cowpland in the 1970s. The latter's innovation would make him one of the greatest inventors of all time.

Despite being such a huge success story, Mike Cowpland has always been available to serve his community. Ottawa-area people constantly bring up his name in his hometown in connection with his many involvements. I'll never forget hearing two local comedians, stage-named Delmer McGregor and Cecil Wiggins, typical country lads with Ottawa Valley twangs, on the car radio one weekday. First, they telephoned the local employment office and, after identifying themselves, asked where they could find executive jobs since their unemployment-assistance cheques were due to run out shortly. The employment counsellor stiffly told them there weren't any executive jobs available for them, but they persisted. When they told him they wanted jobs as vee-pees at Mitel Corporation, he scoffed. Delmer then hung up and immediately called Cowpland, the president of Canada's major hi-tech firm in the Ottawa region, casually posing their question to him.

"Hiya, Mike, this here's Delmer McGregor and Cecil Wiggins," exclaimed Delmer.

"Why, hello Delmer and Cecil, what can I do for you today?"

"Wal Mike, me and Cecil here want jobs 'cause our unemployment cheques are runnin' out, and we figured we could work at yer Mee-tel, especially if ya need a couple of vee-pees. Me and Cecil can do anyting or nuttin' at all. Whattya say?"

Without missing a beat, Cowpland responded, "Of course, boys, come on over and we'll fix you up right away."

Everyone who comes in contact with Mike Cowpland can't help but like him. It's easy to see why.

Michael Cowpland was born on April 23, 1943, in Bexhill, Sussex, England, and after receiving his bachelor of engineering degree from Imperial College at London University in 1964, he emigrated to Canada. At Carleton University in Ottawa, he received his master of science degree in 1968 and his doctor of philosophy degree in 1973. The subject of his dissertation was silicon chip design.

Cowpland began his technical training in 1964 with BNR (Bell Northern Research) as an engineer in product design, leaving the firm in 1968 as a project leader to become manager of circuits design at Microsystems International Limited, where he remained until 1973. At that stage of his career, and of the fortunes of the whole industry, he seized upon the creation and development of what became known as the turning point in leading-edge technology, "the tone-to-pulse converter," a unit that would bridge rotary-telephone equipment with the technology of the future. Together with Terrance Matthews, his brilliant associate from Microsystems International, Cowpland formed Mitel Corporation, and hi-tech communications throughout the world would progress in leaps and bounds from that moment forward.

Cowpland's invention of high-tech hardware and software is legendary, as is his innovative business style, which flourished from seeds planted when he established Mitel Corporation. He served the company as cofounder, president, and CEO from 1973 to 1984 and as chairman in 1985 and 1986.

He and Matthews still joke about Mitel having been made up from Mike and Terry Lawnmower instead of its real derivation: Mike and Terry Electronics. This good-natured humour about such a profound decision is an example of how Cowpland follows his credo to "succeed while having fun." Even at the outset, Mitel Corporation exhibited a company character that was, and still is, the most striking and refreshing in business circles anywhere. A unique open-office concept was designed to greet employees and visitors alike upon entering the company plant in Renfrew, Ontario, where the company would conduct all sizes and kinds of meetings amid informal settings on the wide open main floor, with perimeter walls glassed floor to ceiling, lending an airy expansiveness to the lush and soothing interior complemented by a large circular water fountain in the centre and potted greenery generously strewn about. This was during the late 1970s, when the informality of open shirts and jeans for business attire worn by Mitel personnel was a radical departure from the customary conservative business suits, and it struck a responsive chord with potential employees and clients who were more interested in results than appearances. In fact, this is a clue to the innovative corporate character of Mitel and how the company ultimately became so successful in attracting the kind of amazing talent it wanted to achieve the top-notch performance it expected.

This philosophy still holds true at Corel Corporation, the internationally lauded, award-winning developer and marketer of hi-tech productivity applications, PC graphics, and multimedia software that Cowpland founded in 1985 and of which he is chairman, president, and CEO. Throughout the Corel headquarters established in buildings in Ottawa, Salt Lake City, and Dublin, all personnel are equipped with video telephony at their desks to enable them to have instant, convenient, and constant face-to-face contact with one another despite being located on different floors or even half a world away. And by applying this system to their key clients, personnel can serve their needs right on the spot and save them as well as Corel Corporation an exceptional amount of time, paperwork, freight, personal travel, staff follow-up, and so on by being able to immediately display new products, or witness and diagnose a problem and prescribe a remedy, and set the internal follow-up activities in motion. According to Cowpland, if it weren't for the exceptional efficiencies provided by new high technologies and their applications, Corel would have trouble keeping up with the continually increasing demands of its business. It seems that the hi-tech business is what keeps itself in business!

In high-technology circles, Corel Corporation is well known for its goal-oriented team atmosphere that rewards employees highly. Millions of dollars in awards for exceptional performance, generous employee stock options, and published results of creative achievements are elements of Cowpland's formula for the support of his successful corporate team.

Cowpland believes strongly that only by providing a thoroughly informative climate throughout can Corel expect employees to function properly. This policy is reflected in the weekly *Corel News,* which was initially presented to assembled staff in large conference or theatre facilities. Even though the logistics and costs undertaken for these regular events were substantial, the program proved worthwhile and was expanded into the video-telephony feature program produced internally and telecast every week. A compliance rate of 98 percent shows that this video-on-demand system keeps Corel employees continually "in the loop" even if they have been completely immersed in a project, on the road for awhile, or otherwise engaged. In addition to *Corel News,* training tapes are available on demand through the video-telephony system.

Prominent industry analysts from around the world keep tabs on innovations emanating from Corel Corporation to get a feel for future developments, because Cowpland's predictions are so highly respected. For example, Corel was developing CD-ROMs long before it was clear that the disks would make a serious dent in, much less take over, the market. Today, Corel Corporation markets an impressive slate of software products: CorelDRAW 7, Corel WordPerfect Suite, Corel Office Professional, Corel VENTURA, Corel GALLERY 2, Corel PrintHouse, CorelFLOW 3, CorelVIDEO, and over 300 PhotoCD titles.

Cowpland is currently the holder of 24 essential Canadian patents in the field of high technology. Canada's hi-tech luminary, his wife Marilyn, daughters Paula Christine and Christine Ann, and son Roman reside in the village of Rockcliffe Park near Ottawa.

2

Medical Wonders

The HeartSaver

Tofy Mussivand

Dr. Tofy Mussivand, inventor of the HeartSaver, originally called the EVAD *(for the industry term, "Electrohydraulic Ventricular Assist Device"), is a man of extraordinary vision and depth. As a teenaged boy in the late 1950s, he spent his days contemplating the dilemmas of life . . . and his nights searching the starry heavens for the answers. When I asked for personal details, rather than spending time detailing his life, he excitedly explained the various fundamentals required for designing artificial human replacement organs, and I was soon caught up in his passionate descriptions. Eventually I did receive the background details about Mussivand that I was looking for, and realizing how deeply involved he has been in biomedical-engineering research, development, education, and teaching, I understood why he hadn't wanted to spend time talking about himself, because if he had there wouldn't have*

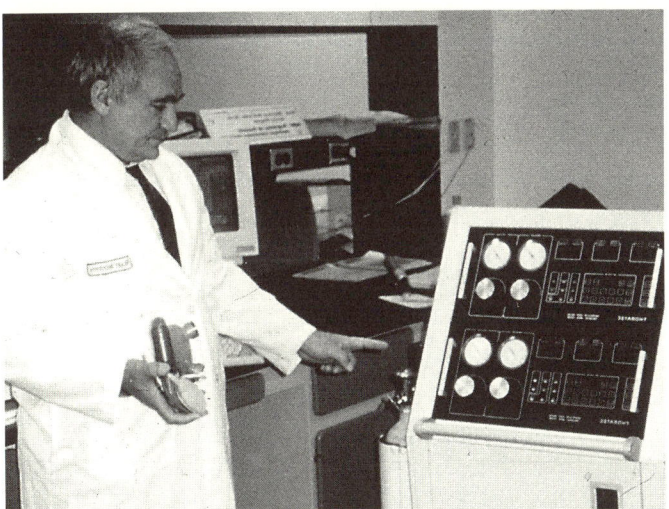

Dr. Tofy Mussivand holding the HeartSaver in his left hand and comparing it to the large console required to drive recent devices. Photo courtesy Cardiovascular Devices Division, University of Ottawa Heart Institute.

been time for much else. I ended up being overwhelmed by the magni-
tude of his science and the uniqueness of his common sense approach.

When Mussivand signalled to me with his silence, his slightly
raised eyebrows, and his hands spread wide that this introductory inter-
view had reached its conclusion, all of his commentary suddenly and
magically fell into place. And then I really began to fathom the signif-
icance of his wonderful invention and how it will affect the life of every
human being on the planet, or at least of those in developed nations
that provide access to such sophisticated medical treatment. And the
driving force behind the HeartSaver project has been a distinguished
alliance of Canadian backers.

It began most probably during the summer of 1957, when a teenaged
Kurd shepherd by the name of Tofy Mussivand watched over a herd
of sheep and goats on the foothill slopes of Mount Ararat, the tallest
mountain of the eastern plateau of Turkey, where, according to the
Bible, Noah's ark came to rest after the great flood. At his father's urg-
ing, introspective young Tofy had studied the Koran, the Old and
New Testaments of the Bible, and other religious teachings in prepa-
ration for priesthood, and he had much to contemplate while tenting
in this lonely region of the Caspian and Black Seas. His interest in
theology and his search for answers finally led to his exciting discovery of a nonreligious knowledge that could answer his questions
about the natural laws of the universe: "How do the stars and the
planets work? What is me? What is you? What is us?" he wondered
to himself. His new knowledge was the science of engineering, and
he marvelled at how it culminated in real solutions. As he pondered
these thoughts, he uncovered more questions to which he needed the
answers, and he began to think about the wonderful ideals that he felt
certain would be able to contribute to the world in the future. To his
great disappointment, he soon found out that his idealistic goal, to
save the world from itself, was not possible, and so he set about to
change his own life instead.

In 1965 Tofy turned 21 and changed countries by emigrating to
Canada, and laughingly he says that he tried to adjust his way of
thinking. He married and thought, "I'll change my wife." He tried, but
he couldn't change her. Then they had children, and he thought, "I'll
change our children." That didn't work either. Finally he thought, "I'll
change myself." And he says that, "when I couldn't even do that, I

simply gave up trying to change people and put my trust into having an inquiring mind to lead me." That decision pointed him toward a career in high technology in relation to the human mind and body and put him on a path to being the creator of a phenomenally significant change: artificial human heart design.

Following successful achievements in engineering, in 1983 Mussivand went on to receive his doctorate in biomedical engineering and medical sciences from the University of Akron and Northwestern Ohio Universities College of Medicine, and he was able to move closer to his early aspirations as a stargazing shepherd living in the open at the foot of Mount Ararat and intently searching for the answers of life. Mussivand began applying the principles of engineering to the human body. He worked with the environmental structure and behaviour of cells, recognizing that they have intelligence that maintains a constant ionic exchange of positive and negative particles – chemical energy, which flows through the membranes separating them. The chemicals within and around cells cause "action potential," electrical voltage commonly measured in the heart by ECG and in the brain by EEG. Mussivand considers that each cell in the human body acts like a battery, constantly charging and recharging. These are all natural physical principles used in engineering, and they are applied to the structure and function of the human body.

Moreover, the healthy cell environment maintains pH balance, temperature, and composition of gases, all within specific ranges, but if the environment is not within these ranges, it spells trouble for the health of the human being. With all of this interaction taking place, Mussivand then postulated the existence of the universal prime mover, for it can only be God who ordains the intelligence that enables each cell to respond to pleasure or distress. We have our minds to tell us when we feel something and to decide to react, but who or what tells cells to respond to changes in environment? Mussivand believes that, beyond any religious reasoning, the prime mover is inexorably part of the equation, and for him this reasonable conclusion ends the traditional debate between creationists and scientists.

Mussivand didn't realize that artificial human organs were a possibility until he was exposed to work being conducted at the

Cleveland Clinic, where he saw an artificial human heart for the first time. However, the device was a heavy steel cabinet on wheels and could hardly offer a normal life to the patient hooked up to it. It was then that the pioneer artificial-organ surgeon Dr. Yukihiko Nosé, who had studied under the renowned inventor of the dialysis machine, or artificial kidney, Dr. Willem Kolff, asked Dr. Mussivand if he could assist in the development of an artificial heart. Mussivand reviewed all of the technology related to artificial-heart development, including that of many other countries, and was able to conclude that over $400 million of intense research and development work to date had not resulted in success, compelling the little shepherd in Tofy to ask, "Why?"

An intense regimen of research, in which Mussivand read hundreds of case examinations and mountains of medical papers published in Canada and abroad, culminated in a monumental breakthrough when he established rudimentary design criteria for the EVAD. After this painstaking research and development, Mussivand was able to enumerate seven reasons why the medical development of a thoroughly successful artificial heart had been confounded for so many years: (1) anatomical compatibility; (2) the need for remote power to eliminate infection from wires through the skin and to enhance appearance, cleanliness, and mobility for the patient, instead of being hooked up to a massive 300-pound machine; (3) remote, noninvasive monitoring via satellite and control by telecommunications signals to the device while in use by the patient, anywhere in the world; (4) the complete assurance of tissue compatibility to avoid toxicity, burning, and clotting; (5) the need to dramatically improve the patient's daily quality of life rather than simply delaying death; (6) reasonable affordability; and (7) the general acceptance of the artificial heart by the public.

Only the passionate devotion of an ingenious medical engineer could come to grips with this formidable challenge, and Dr. Tofy Mussivand has successfully resolved the seven issues and requirements that have so thoroughly baffled medical science. These solutions are patented throughout the world, and wide international attraction to the HeartSaver is taking place, indicating the existence of vast potential in markets expected to strive to reduce deaths due to heart failure: 45,000 annually in Canada, 500,000 in the United

States, and an enormous 4 million worldwide.

The World Heart Corporation was established to undertake responsibility for further research and development, financing, and marketing. As president, Dr. Mussivand leads the research and development program as chief operating officer; prominent heart surgeon Dr. Wilbert Keon is chairman of the Clinical Advisory Committee; owner of the Ottawa Senators of the National Hockey League, Corel Centre owner, and high-tech entrepreneur Rod Bryden is chairman and CEO; and Corel Corporation chairman and CEO Dr. Michael Cowpland provides the major financial support and serves on the World Heart Corporation board of directors.

According to Bryden, "Ventricular Assist Devices (VADs) have been proven successful in supporting blood circulation for people with failing hearts. Thousands of people are alive today because of this successful technology. The collateral effects on the user have, until now, made use of the devices attractive only for a brief time and for a small percentage of people suffering from heart failure. The HeartSaver is the first VAD that is fully implantable in the chest, remotely powered, monitored, and controlled, leaving the user without holes in the skin or the diaphragm. We believe the HeartSaver will be attractive to thousands of people who suffer from heart failure and who would, without a VAD, face deterioration of their vital organs and ultimately death. The HeartSaver is expected to deliver proven VAD circulatory support without the negative collateral effects on the user."

Mussivand has academic appointments at the Department of Surgery, Faculty of Medicine, University of Ottawa, and at the Department of Mechanical and Aerospace Engineering, Faculty of Engineering, Carleton University. He teaches courses in biomedical engineering, systems engineering, and management at the University of Ottawa and Carleton University. He also supervises resident graduate students from several universities, including, among others, Carleton University, the University of Ottawa, Berlin University, and Berufsakademi Ravensburg (Germany). He has published over 100 papers, books, and reports and holds patents for outstanding inventions: Unified System Ventricular Assist Device, Minimum Invasive Surgery, In Vitro Hematological Test Circuit, and Remote Biotelemetry.

The Pacemaker Saga

John Hopps

For over a month, I telephoned the local number I had for John Hopps, the renowned inventor of the heart pacemaker, hoping to talk to him about his remarkable innovation. I tried to reach him at various times of the day and on different weekdays, but all I heard was a ringing phone in an empty house. Obviously there was no one at home. Had he gone south for the winter? How was I going to locate and interview him in time to meet my deadline for this book?

Luckily I was directed to his son Don, and the evening that I dropped in at his home he was preparing to visit his father the next day at his winter home in Florida. As a financial analyst with Health Canada, Don is very much a part of the medical community, and he appreciated my situation. After I explained that I planned to write about his father and needed his help to find and interview him, Don smiled and offered his assistance. His eagerness to help reminded me that when I had asked people at the National Research Council and the University of Ottawa Heart Institute for help in determining the whereabouts of the inventor of the pacemaker, they had responded in much the same way as Don did. This response was a clue of the awesome impact that Hopps's invention has made.

Through his son, I was able to locate John Hopps in Florida and both he and Don provided me with the information for this story.

John Hopps was born in Winnipeg in 1919 and showed a remarkable propensity for study and detail as an accomplished writer at a very young age. When he was a 10-year-old choirboy, he wrote the monthly *Choir News* for his church; a few years later, when he was a boy scout, he edited *Taurus* magazine. In 1941, at 21 years of age, John obtained his degree in electrical engineering from the University of Manitoba and went immediately to the National Research Council in Ottawa. There he began an inspirational career during which he devoted much time to developing cardiovascular instrumentation, which today helps to keep legions of people around the world alive. In an incredible stroke of irony, the very device that he developed would be implanted in his own chest some 30 years later, in 1985, to keep his heart ticking with regularity.

At the NRC John worked on diverse innovative engineering projects that were proposed to shore up research and development needed by private industry. He immersed himself in the study of radio-frequency heating and conducted a wide assortment of experiments. He had built a 2,000-watt oscillator and was working on various applications, including furniture glues, beer pasteurization, and honey. "It became my gateway to the future," he explains.

In 1949 the University of Toronto commenced a study of hypothermia and conscripted John from the NRC to join medical scientists at the Banting Institute in Toronto for a week each month to work on the application of radio-frequency heating to restore body temperature, and this project was his introduction to an association that continued for many years.

One of his eminent colleagues in the Cardiovascular Laboratory of the Banting Institute, Dr. Wilfred Bigelow, observed during a

Dr. John Hopps, 1968.
Photo courtesy National Research Council of Canada.

hypothermia experiment with a lab animal that the heart stopped when muscular contraction failed at a low temperature. When he prodded the left ventricle, the heart muscle contracted. He poked again, and the heart beat again. He found that when the heart was artificially stimulated, it behaved in a normal fashion, but when he ceased the stimulation, the heart also stopped. The application of electricity also produced the same results. Following manual cardiac massage, the animal was resuscitated and recovered.

With his amazing discovery, Bigelow had opened the door to the innovation that would revolutionize cardiac treatment from that time forward: the development of the pacemaker by Dr. John Hopps.

Study of the literature revealed that in 1936 a Dr. Sweet had used repetitive electrical bursts to produce a heartbeat in human hearts after they had stopped completely, but nothing further of this phenomenon had been studied. In addition, Hopps noted that in the 1930s the respected physiologist Carl Wiggers had conducted many experiments along these lines with animals, and since 1932 Dr. William Kouwenhoven had reported on defibrillation using electrical shocks. Also, Dr. Claude Beck was developing a clinical application of electrical stimulation along with suction massage to the exposed heart during surgery at Western Reserve University in Cleveland.

Hopps returned to his NRC laboratory to produce a pacemaker that would fire single electrical pulses at appropriate rates to control a heart at normal or lowered temperature. His instrument combined a defibrillator with the pacer to shock a heart in uncoordinated contractions back to a normal rhythm.

During early 1950 in the NRC laboratory, the first human heart pacemaker was built. It was the era of vacuum tubes, before the advent of the transistor, and the device was large and therefore could not be implanted in the chest. However, this prototype led to continuing research on energy requirements and optimal pulse forms that have found application in today's implantable units.

In the early 1950s, Hopps's group at the NRC built prototypes and supplied a number of them, complete with detailed procedural information, to at least 10 locations in the United States. (In 1957, patent rights were granted to a surgeon in the U.S.) They also scouted the Canadian scene for a potential manufacturer and made an arrangement with Smith and Stone Limited, manufacturer of their sophisticated electrocardioscope, which produced some early models. The first pacemaker was implanted in a human body in 1958.

The pacemaker developments were followed by other cardiovascular instruments. Hopps would be exasperated for several years in his attempts to work with private Canadian industry to market the outstanding yet highly innovative device. He was working on the design of a mobile cardiac resuscitation cart for the Banting group, containing rewarming equipment, a heart rate meter, a blood pressure monitor, an electrocardioscope, and an oxygen resuscitator. Named the "tea wagon" at the NRC, the cart dominated activities there until the complex innovation was finally ready for clinical use.

At that point, in 1957, Hopps accepted an offer to serve as a consulting engineer for one year at the Ministry of Health in Ceylon in order to organize a Department of Electromedical Engineering. Throughout the 1960s and 1970s, he continually contributed innovative creations through the NRC and set about to inspire various segments of Canadian society, including aspiring medical scientists, through a rigorous schedule of speaking engagements, during which he was a strong advocate for standards in the design and production of electrical installations in health care facilities.

John A. Hopps, OC, B.Sc.E.E., P.Eng., D. Sc., headed the Committee for Electrical Safety of Medical Equipment, chaired the CSA Standards Committee on Electrical Installations in Health Care Facilities, was founding president of the Canadian Medical and Biological Engineering Society, president and later secretary general of the International Federation for Medical and Biological Engineering, and secretary general of the International Union of

Underside view of Model 4 Stimulator-Defibrillator, an early forerunner of the pacemaker.
Photo courtesy National Research Council of Canada.

Physics and Engineering in Science and Medicine.

In recognition of his development of the pacemaker and his services to the profession, the University of Manitoba conferred on Hopps the degree of doctor of science in 1976. The North American Society of Pacing and Electrophysiology honoured Dr. Hopps along with Drs. Bigelow and Callaghan with the 1985 Distinguished Scientist Award for their development of the pacemaker. Also in 1985 Hopps received the IEEE Region 7 Award and the A.C.L. McNaughton Medal for outstanding contribution to electrical and electronics engineering, and in June 1986 he was awarded the Order of Canada for his contributions to the sciences in Canada. In 1987 he was accorded the Biomedical Engineering Leadership Award in the United States.

Hopps has written a book about his career, and it is available by order from Dr. John A. Hopps, c/o CMBES Secretariat, 134 – 837 Eastvale Drive, Gloucester, Ontario, Canada KIJ 7T5.

The Anywhere, Two-Minute Blood Analysis Device

Imant Lauks

Just by looking at Imant Lauks comfortably lounging back in his chair during my interview, gazing introspectively into space and poking at the air with his pencil as though he were a musical conductor, you'd never know he worked in such a pressure cooker. This was a Tuesday morning, and he'd just returned from meetings in New York the day before, had met three scientists from New Jersey who had dropped by his office to announce that they were ready for their meeting as soon as he was, and was even then preparing for another trip before the end of the week. It was obvious that Imant thrives on the pressure, but now he was relaxed and seemed to relish being able to look back upon his innovative career. You could tell this was far from his usual intense focusing of attention on the future of our evolving society, an orientation he uses to direct his own work, as well as the activities of his firm's 200 technical professionals.

Imant shook his head and grinned. "You know," he said, "everybody's still waiting for that glorious information highway dream that would give us everything and make life so easy. And we expected so much that even when we get a lot we think it's only a little. The thing is, we have it all now!" Thanks to the Imant Laukses of the world, we sure do.

Born in 1952 in Bradford, an industrial town in northern England, of hard-working Latvian parents, Imant Lauks was raised in the Latvian community and speaks fondly of his cultural teachings. His mother Rita was in home-furnishings sales, and his father Roland left mining coal to run his own delicatessen for a number of years before joining a deli-food importer-distributor as a salesman. Imant's brother Karl is one year older. Imant is the inventor in the family.

He earned his bachelor of science degree in chemistry in 1973 and his doctorate in electrical engineering in 1977 from Imperial College at

London University. The title of his dissertation was "Chemical Reactions at Zinc Oxide Surface," which covers the general area of his future innovative investigations and inventions. He was then appointed professor of electrical engineering at the University of Pennsylvania, and even then he thought that his key advantage was having formal education in two disciplines. By then Imant was 25 years of age. He met his future wife Rita in Toronto, where they were married.

"Hi-tech invention is in stark contrast to the usual process which is engaged to create products in our regular living environment," Imant explains. "By nature hi-tech or biotech innovations are systems oriented, requiring a wide amalgam of talent with a cast of sometimes hundreds of technical professionals in various disciplines whose efforts need to be funnelled toward a common cause and supported by large amounts of money over a number of years. Often, to achieve something of lasting value in high technology, a lot of things need to be done, and done right, which requires the building of a large organization, raising a large amount of money."

Imant spoke of a typical example of $200 million ($100 million to develop the technology, and $100 million to develop the market) having been invested in a single project that, at this point in its 14 years, has not yet generated its potential income . . . but it will. It all boils down to the need for considerable up-front investment, but the returns are also great. In order to achieve this magnitude of returns, an attractive and sizeable market is necessary, and for that market to be adequate, it must be worldwide. Further to meeting investment demands, the ultimate challenge is to invent a widely and realistically useful product, then to assemble the development group and provide an environment in which everyone can work and create together. Experience tells Imant that out of 100 hi-tech companies, five are likely to get to the public-offering stage, and only one will eventually make it to producing a product with lasting value and will actually earn money doing it.

Imant believes in sound basic research that comes from attentive study of the environment related to a specific problem that he is trying to resolve. It's very important for him to know exactly what the problem is and to see for himself how the user copes with every detail of the technology.

Imant's invention of the i-Stat system simplifies the process of blood analysis. His design combines silicon chip technology with traditional electrochemistry and offers handheld portability and nearly instantaneous blood analysis without sacrificing an iota of accuracy and reliability. So, rather than having to wait for many hours or even days for blood test results, in less than two minutes (with just a few drops of whole blood) critical test results can be obtained and addressed immediately. The handheld i-Stat device can do 12 of the most common blood tests, many of which are required in critical care.

Blood tests can be used for diagnosing symptoms, for monitoring a patient's course of therapy or during a procedure performed on a patient, or for a medical checkup. The values in the body can change significantly over a period of hours, as they are likely to when a patient is in medical distress, so the shorter the time taken for results, the greater the value in the test.

In the case of tiny, 1,000-gram babies in neonatal care, who have a limited supply of blood, the i-Stat system reduces the amount of blood needed for testing. As a result there is a reduced need for transfusions. Hospital studies show that i-Stat blood testing shortens a patient's length of stay in emergency by 90 minutes. Hospitals also use it to monitor neonatal and pediatric patients during transport. Most of these patients are placed on ventilators during travel, and before i-Stat there was no way to monitor their blood. The system is generally credited with paving the way for treatment to begin sooner, which can make the difference between life and death.

The i-Stat system is comprised of an analyzer unit and cartridges. Each single-use cartridge, which performs a series of blood tests, is equipped with a collection device for a few drops of blood to be channelled into contact with one or more solid-state chips containing different chemicals and biological components that react in a defined way to things in the blood that need to be measured. The result of each reaction emits an electrical signal that is transmitted to the battery-powered analyzer unit and interpreted on its liquid crystal display screen. At this point the digitized information is communicated via infrared link to the information network serving the patient, such as a hospital, a clinic, or even a space station . . . literally anywhere.

The quest for the i-Stat system began in 1986 with what Imant terms his "vision statement," a hand-drawn image of his concept from which he was able to work. From there he and the i-Stat technology team developed the chip technology and the design rules for product engineering, and when the analyzer unit and cartridges were eventually built, and the required series of clinical trials was conducted, i-Stat finally entered the marketplace in 1992. The process from launch to market took more than six years, including concept gestation.

In 1995, Hewlett-Packard of Palo Alto, California, made a $61-million investment in i-Stat Corporation and is currently marketing i-Stat internationally. The i-Stat system joins an impressive portfolio of other Hewlett-Packard medical monitoring devices being marketed around the world, from ultrasound machines to magnetic resonance imaging (MRI) machines.

In time the i-Stat system will be in general use throughout the world, and even beyond this world, as it is now part of the medical monitoring procedures employed by NASA and the Russian space station MIR.

Dr. Imant R. Lauks is founder, chief technology officer, and executive vice president of i-Stat Canada Limited in Kanata, Ontario. He currently holds 14 Canadian patents for electrical engineering and chemical inventions. He and Rita, his wife of 20 years, and their three daughters Lacy, Sasha, and Becky live in the village of Rockcliffe Park, Ontario.

Astronaut performing blood tests in space. Note the floating i-Stat analyzer in zero gravity.
Photo courtesy NASA.

3

Sporting Innovators

The Man Who
Invented Basketball

James Naismith

Basketball has become such a prominent professional sport since I played the game back in high school that it's utterly amazing to me how a person could have been such a visionary to have invented this rather intricate indoor game over 100 years ago in 1891. However, after I met the people who now carry Dr. James Naismith's banner so conscientiously, I have a glimmer of how great this man was and of how he actually achieved his greatness. My synopsis of his accomplishments is the result of interviews with Naismith's descendants, friends who are still living, and the staff at the Dr. James Naismith Centre, which is located on the farm where he grew up. It should not have surprised me that his personal warmth and goodwill fairly bubbled from these people, for Naismith never personally exploited any of his creations by the usual patent process because he considered that they were gifts to be freely enjoyed by everyone. And during my research, I felt as though he were still alive to constantly remind everyone he knew to be kind and gentle whenever they represent him. I could not help but be similarly impressed with the memory of this wonderful man and his gifts to the world, and I hope that I convey a sense of this generous character in his story.

Dr. James Naismith – athlete, inventor, medical doctor, preacher, professor, and administrator – contributed a legacy of fair play and good sportsmanship to organized sport around the world, as well as being the originator of the highly popular indoor game of basketball.

Of Scottish descent, Naismith was born in 1861 in Bennie's Corners, a hamlet of 75 people in eastern Ontario near Almonte. In 1869 his father found more work in his trade as a carpenter and lumberman on Grand Calumet Island in the Ottawa River some 70 miles away and moved his family there. But by late 1870, both his father and mother had died of typhoid fever and, along with his brother and sister, young Jimmy was taken by his mother's relatives to their home just outside the thriving village of Almonte, across a gully from the original homestead where he had been born nine years earlier.

From a young age, James developed a love of sports and demonstrated his emerging character, distinguished by an inherent kindness and a high regard for the welfare of others, especially in the realm of sport. Since he was blessed with a sturdy physique, he was well known to excel at each of the many sports he played, including rugby, football, lacrosse, baseball, cricket, curling, gymnastics, and track and field activities. His early resourcefulness was noted when he made his own ice skates out of some old wood files that he shaped and sharpened on a grindstone and set into strips of hickory to strap onto his boots. Then he was able to enjoy winter fun and games with his friends without having to ask for the money to buy new skates.

At one point James dropped out of high school for several years to work in logging camps in winter and on the farm in summer so that he could contribute to the support of his orphaned sister and brother as well as himself by working for their guardian. The constant regimen of outdoor hard labour toughened Jim psychologically as well as physically, but apparently he seemed to have "found" himself at one point and returned to graduate from high school. After graduation he was accepted into McGill University in Montreal, where he completed his bachelor of arts degree (honours) in philosophy and Hebrew and placed in the top 10 of his class. His studies continued with another three years at Montreal's Presbyterian College and two years at the International YMCA Teacher Training School in Massachusetts. Almost overnight Jim became a varsity football star, and during all these years of study he never missed playing in a single game. Not bad going for a previous high school dropout!

It was during his stint in Massachusetts that James faced the challenge of creating a new game for his students to play in the gymnasium. The criteria for the game required that it be an indoor winter sport and that it have no body contact. Capitalizing on some of the aspects of the Duck-on-a-Rock game that he had played on the farm as a child, Jim's creation would end up being one of the most popular organized and competitive sports in the world.

In Duck-on-a-Rock, one player's fist-sized stone, acting as the "duck," would be placed on a large flat boulder as the target for the other players, who would attempt to score by hitting the "duck" with their stones. Because the goal area was somewhat out of reach, the usual body contact used in most sports to protect the goal was eliminated. This was the concept that Jim used, and he placed the two goals up in the air, out of reach of the players, and used peach baskets to catch the scoring balls. With a framework of regulations aimed at the further elimination of body contact, the sport of basketball was born. The date was December 21, 1891.

Sporting a cauliflower ear from constant football injuries, James attempted to protect his ears from being ripped off while playing football by flattening them with wide adhesive tape. By using several layers of flannel fastened under his chin, he found that the protection improved and tried to ignore the derision and laughter from the other players, who thought that he looked uproariously funny. He then replaced the flannel with chamois, and apparently he didn't look so funny. Finally, by using a football cut in half, a rudimentary football helmet was born. Improvements in design and fabrication over the years have resulted in the modern football helmet, the most significant protection device in the game, and the one that has likely spared this potentially brutal sport from being cancelled by legislators.

On April 8, 1898, at the age of 37, Naismith obtained his doctor of medicine degree from Gross Medical College of Rocky Mountain University in Denver. In September of that year, he made the career move of his life to Lawrence, Kansas, where he took his young wife Maude and their first two daughters of an eventual brood of five children. There, at the University of Kansas, he initially coached basketball, track, and fencing (including the broadsword), and he remained a Canadian citizen until after World War I.

In the mid-1930s, young John McLendon was attracted to Naismith's innovative program, which offered a bachelor of science degree in physical education. But John, the only black student in the class, wasn't supposed to play or coach basketball because of the racial barriers of the time. Naismith routed John around these barriers, enabling him to become such a fine basketball coach that he was eventually inducted into the Naismith Memorial Hall of Fame in

Springfield, Massachusetts. When Naismith asked John what he intended to do after graduation, John explained that he couldn't afford to continue university studies. Naismith sat him down in his office while he called the University of Iowa and landed him a job in statistics to put him through for his master's degree in physical education. Today McLendon says, "As soon as we met, Dr. Naismith changed my whole life, and he also did this for many, many others... He was always doing a lot of things for a lot of people. I know that Dr. Naismith's lifelong dream was fully realized when basketball became recognized as an official Olympic sport at the 1936 Olympics in Germany. The population of Lawrence also raised money in a North America-wide fund-raising effort to send Dr. and Mrs. Naismith to the Olympics, and when he paid me 50 cents for mowing his lawn, I handed it right back to him as my donation."

After retiring from the University of Kansas in 1937, Naismith still taught part-time and enjoyed fishing when visiting his boyhood home in Almonte. From when he moved to Lawrence until he passed away in 1939, Dr. James Naismith, originally an impoverished Canadian orphan from the backwoods of eastern Ontario, enriched the world of sport with what has stemmed from his wonderful invention – towering sport heroes such as Magic Johnson and Michael Jordan, sensational teams such as the Knicks, the Bulls, and the Raptors, new meanings for words such as dribbling, and new words for meanings such as slam-dunk!

In Almonte the Dr. James Naismith Basketball Foundation Visitor and Information Centre receives people from May through Thanksgiving each year. There is a Naismith Drive in both Gloucester and Almonte, Ontario, as well as in Lawrence,

Dr. James Naismith, a true sportsman.
Photo by Duke D'Ambra, circa 1936. Courtesy Dr. James Naismith Basketball Foundation, Almonte, Ontario.

Kansas. A permanent Dr. James Naismith memorial portrait is on display in Allen Field House in Lawrence, and there is the Naismith memorial marker at Eighth and Kentucky Streets. A private dormitory at the University of Kansas is named for him, there is a large granite setting at Naismith Memorial Gardens in Memorial Park Cemetery in East Lawrence, the American Football Hall of Fame in Canton, Ohio, pays tribute to his invention of the football helmet, and dedications to his memory linking past with present basketball glories are maintained by the Naismith Basketball Hall of Fame in Springfield, Massachusetts.

THE CRADLE OF HOCKEY
Nova Scotia

Was hockey born in the early 1800s on Long Pond near Windsor, Nova Scotia? Dr. Sandy Young, a sports historian at Dalhousie University in Halifax, stated, "We do know it grew out of other games, the Scottish game of shinty, Irish hurling and English bandy." Furthermore, Young's book Beyond Heroes: A Sport History of Nova Scotia *contends that a form of hockey was played in Windsor, Nova Scotia, during the early 1800s. Some historians propose that Native Americans first played hockey on this continent.*

People who've written about the birthplace of hockey and how the game originated like to think of the sport as having been invented by the gods and placed on Earth for everyone to enjoy. I appreciate that sentiment, but I think that we should give credit to the mostly anonymous innovators who, so many years ago, shaped our great national pastime. The people who have steadfastly kept the story alive, especially Howard Dill, also deserve appreciation and support.

The first recorded reference to "hurley-on-ice" in Canada, considered the precursor of hockey, was written by Supreme Court Judge Thomas Chandler Haliburton, who was also a noted author. His book *The Attaché; or, Sam Slick in England,* published in two series in 1844 in London, England, contained some Sam Slick wisdoms that became part of the English vocabulary and are commonly used in conversation even today: Don't look a gift horse in the mouth; A stitch in time saves nine; Seeing is believing; Quick as a wink; The early bird gets the worm; and Truth is stranger than fiction. His book is also the first written history of Nova Scotia, and in it Haliburton recalls his childhood as a student boarding at King's Collegiate, now King's-Edgehill School, in Windsor, Nova Scotia, where hurley-on-ice was a favourite winter pastime: ". . . boys let out racin', yelpin', hollerin', and whoopin' like mad with pleasure . . . [playing] hurley on the long pond on the ice, or campin' out anight at the Chester lakes to fish." This dates hurley-on-ice on Long Pond at about the year 1800. Having been handed down through many generations of the Dill family since then, Long Pond is located on Howard Dill's farm property, which borders the King's-Edgehill School campus.

In the early days, the students maintained the ice themselves, and because of the absence of outdoor lighting, they had to stop playing a while before dark in order to hike home through the woods that wound past Frog Pond and Devil's Punch Bowl, where they went skating at times. The story about playing this exciting game on ice spread quickly when the King's Collegiate students returned to their hometowns in Annapolis, Halifax, St. John, and other parts of the Maritimes, as well as in Ontario, England, Scotland, Ireland, the United States, and Spain, and introduced it to their friends there.

In Halifax and nearby Dartmouth, the boys became just as excited about playing hurley-on-ice as the Windsor boys, and the game soon dominated their winter activities too. The game became so popular that it interfered with church attendance and Sunday school, so much so that many parents along with the clergy were against it. Gradually the game evolved and was sometimes called "ricket" or "hurley" or "hockey," and its popularity grew and grew. "Hockey" is an ancient English word for field hockey, a rough-and-tumble game played in muddy fields; it is also an English family name. According to local legend in the Windsor area, a Colonel Hockey stationed at Fort Edward required his troops to exercise with a game that eventually took his name. Another explanation offered for the name comes from the French word for a shepherd's crook, *hoquet,* but this hypothesis lacks credibility.

Samuel Cameron was born in Scotland in 1814 and, after serving with the Royal Highland Immigrants in Quebec, received a farmland grant in Pictou County, Nova Scotia. While playing hurley-on-ice on the East River, he injured his knee and its condition worsened to the extent that he was forced to give up farming completely and revert to teaching school instead.

A reporter for the *Colonial Patriot* in Pictou referred to the game of hurley as break-shins in 1829. The *Nova Scotian* in Halifax reported news in 1831 of skating parties on the North West Arm and of a game of "wicket" played there. In 1833 the *Colonial Patriot* proclaimed that hurley was being played with great enthusiasm by coal miners in Pictou. In 1842 the *Halifax Morning Post* wrote that "ricket" was a popular game being played on frozen lakes around Dartmouth.

In 1859 a reporter from the *Boston Evening Gazette* wrote about his discovery of the game during a visit to Halifax. The next year the Prince of Wales visited Windsor, Halifax, and Boston, and in 1863 he is reported to have played ice hockey at his home in England. When the Starr self-fastening skates were invented in Dartmouth, boys for miles around began playing hockey on Starr Acme Club skates.

Lacrosse was being heavily promoted in Montreal and Toronto around 1867 as Canada's national game, and organizers were sent out to the east coast and to England. In Halifax, Lacrosse was played on ice, as it was played in Montreal by members of the Montreal Football Club, but it was abandoned in favour of the much more popular ice hockey. During all this time, the game continued to develop and was called various names, but the name hurley, from which it originated, remained dominant.

According to the Windsor Heritage Hockey Society, documented proof shows that James Creighton of Halifax introduced hockey to Montreal, where the first organized game was played in a rink on March 3, 1875. Other records reveal that in 15 years hockey had spread to the west coast, with reports of games being played in Winnipeg and Victoria in 1890.

Throughout this period the basic rules of hockey evolved, as did the equipment. Pucks were customarily wooden slices of an appropriately sized hardwood sapling. The sticks, called hurleys in early times and later on hockeys, were originally made by Micmac Indians according to their special design for *alchamadajk,* the Micmac name for hurley-on-ice, although it was in 1900 that James Leggatt of Hamilton, Ontario, was first to patent the hockey stick. And the skates were, of course, made by Starr in Dartmouth.

As hockey became nationally recognized, it came in from the cold to be organized and played in covered ice rinks from coast to coast. In 1899 the Nova Scotia box net was invented, and the new century began with hockey fully established and popular across the country. It had become the Canadian national pastime.

In researching his book *King's-Edgehill School: 1788-1988,* in commemoration of the school's bicentennial anniversary in 1988, Leslie

Loomer uncovered early references to hockey on Long Pond. In 1876 the *Windsor Mail* included a series called "Early Sketches of Windsor," which are now in a scrapbook in the Nova Scotia Public Archives. The anonymous writer described what student life was like at King's Collegiate during his stay from 1816 to 1818: "The Devil's Punch Bowl and Long Pond, back of the College, were favourite resorts, and we used to skate in winter, on moonlight nights, on the ponds. I recollect John Cunard (brother of Sir Samuel, of steamship fame) having his front teeth knocked out with a hurley by Pete Delancey of Annapolis."

Montreal sportswriter and broadcaster Elmer Ferguson stated that after "probing into maritime hockey lore, I am satisfied that ice hockey really began in Nova Scotia." And Brian McFarlane, the host of *Hockey Night in Canada* for 27 years and the author of many books on hockey, declared, "In all my years of doing research into the origins of the game, I have never seen anything documented about the first game of hurley or hockey being played on ice until I saw the evidence that Thomas Chandler Haliburton of Windsor recorded regarding the game being played by students of King's College School on Long Pond circa 1800. I know of no place in Canada where there is any

Howard Dill, fifth generation of the Dill family to own Long Pond, now Steel Pond, Nova Scotia, where the game of ice hockey is believed to have first been played around 1800. He's holding a pair of antique ice skates. Photo courtesy Howard Dill.

written evidence of the game being played any earlier. Since hockey developed from hurley-on-ice in Nova Scotia, until there is such evidence [from elsewhere], I endorse and support the claim of Windsor, Nova Scotia, to the birthplace of the wonderful game of hockey."

The Windsor Hockey Heritage Society has compiled a list of important dates in ice hockey history:

1800	Hurley-on-ice began in Windsor, Nova Scotia.
1800-59	Hurley developed into ice hockey in Nova Scotia.
1875	Organized hockey began in Montreal.
1886	Organized hockey began in Kingston.
1890	Hockey spread across Canada.
1893	The Stanley Cup was presented by Lord Stanley in Ontario.
1896	The Starr Trophy was presented by the Starr Skate Company in Nova Scotia.
1899	Nova Scotians used fish net over goal posts to form the "box net."
1900s	The box net was first used in Toronto.
1900	The Citizen's Trophy, Windsor's first trophy, was handed out.
1901	The box net became popular across Canada.
1917	The NHL was formed.

Making Hockey Safer

Tom Pashby

Hockey is the greatest game in the world to play and to watch. Just ask Murray Costello, the president of the Canadian Hockey Association (CHA, formerly the CAHA), the organization responsible for 530,000 youngsters registered in hockey programs across Canada. Murray hears it all the time from parents or hockey greats reminiscing about playing hockey after school or in the evening, passing the puck, shooting goals, racing along the ice and enjoying the rush of air, and crashing into the corners struggling for possession of the puck. It's the fastest game on earth, and it's made to be rough. The average player fires a slapshot at 22 metres per second and can move at a blistering speed with stick and skates flashing in a blur. That's on the upside.

On the downside there's a terrible toll of blinded eyes and smashed faces taken for all this fun. That is, until Dr. Tom Pashby came along and, with his brand of firm yet gentle persuasion, made people take stock of what was happening to this wonderful game and put a stop to the carnage.

Pashby started by protecting youngsters in minor hockey from serious eye injuries, and by today he has achieved success throughout all age groups, in some of the other physically risky sports as well, and set the example that is being followed around the world. Although protective masks and helmets have "tamed" rough sports such as hockey, he believes that "It's just a matter of time" before further innovations bring back any lost excitement by being much lighter and less intrusive than the present gear, which is nonetheless far better than the protective equipment first introduced. And by establishing an environment for constant review via a CSA certification committee, Pashby has made certain that the sport invites inventors to contribute their improvements in concept, design, and materials.

It has been almost 60 years since Pashby first argued for a safer environment for sports such as hockey, but now there is a viable new industry, based upon his innovative guidance, to manufacture and market various types of eye and face protectors. He didn't get much sup-port at the beginning. But with a hard-hitting campaign using reliable facts and figures, and ultimately patient cajoling over the years, he has been able to build on each of his little successes. And what is his reward? Pashby says that "the great feeling I have every day is all the compensation I'd ever want."

That's Dr. Tom Pashby, all right.

Before he became an eye physician and surgeon, Tom Pashby was shocked into concern over eye injuries in sport when a friend suffered a severe eye injury during a game in Maple Leaf Gardens. It was in November 1939 that George Parsons, a player for the Toronto Maple Leafs, was struck in the left eye when an opponent raised his stick to attempt a check and hit him with it by accident. His eye was damaged so severely that it had to be removed, and his dashing hockey career was done forever. When he witnessed this accident, Tom was in his final year of medical school and an avid hockey fan and amateur player, and the gruesome event left an indelible impression on the budding young doctor.

Born in Toronto on March 23, 1915, Tom loved hockey from an early age, playing with buddies in Riverdale, in the city's east end. The bunch included future Toronto Maple Leafs hockey greats Bob Davidson and Jim Fowler, and there was Don Somerville, the future Toronto mayor who died on the ice in the 1950s while playing goal. And he was only in his forties.

After Tom Pashby graduated from medical school and completed a general internship, he enlisted in the RCAF, in which he spent the remainder of the war. With the war and his discharge behind him, Pashby completed ophthalmological training. After attending every Maple Leafs home game in a season and getting to know many of the players and the club doctors, he was asked to see injured players as well as their families. Soon he was the unofficial eye consultant to the hockey club, and he continued in this role through the 1950s and 1960s. He also spent Saturday evenings sewing up facial cuts at the local arena. He would bring two or three suturing kits from the Toronto Sick Children's Hospital (where he was on staff) to the rink and never failed to make use of them during the five games each night. "Suturing a laceration immediately requires no anesthesia," Dr.

Pashby explains, "but waiting to have the suturing done in hospital was painful. This was another reason for my deepening concern over the need for face protectors, not just eye protectors."

History repeated itself during a game in Maple Leaf Gardens in 1952, when another good friend of Pashby's, Herb Dickenson, while playing for the New York Rangers, was hit in the right eye by a puck. Tom accompanied him to the hospital, and despite having surgery the eye was left with only "counting-fingers" vision. As had happened to George Parsons, it was also Herb's last hockey game.

In 1959 Tom's eldest son Bill, then 14 years old, suffered a severe head injury while playing house league hockey. However, luck was with him, and he recovered fully, but the seed was planted in Tom's mind and years later resulted in his promoting the acceptance of good helmet design.

Pashby was very busy with his eye practice during the following 20 years, all the while becoming more and more disgusted by the deplorable record of mounting eye injuries in sport, particularly in hockey. He was especially upset that these serious eye injuries were being suffered by youngsters while playing organized minor league hockey games or even recreational hockey on community rinks. Because young hockey players were becoming bigger and stronger, and were receiving better and more intensive training, eye and head injuries were becoming much more common and more serious with every passing year.

The costs of eye and facial injuries in hockey can be staggering. It can cost $250,000 and more in hospital and medical bills for a severely damaged eye, and the personal effects from facial injury can be devastating. Pashby has seen many cases in which players have had to look for new careers after losing the sight in an eye during a hockey game.

Then, in November 1973, a talented junior player on the Toronto Marlboroughs, Greg Neeld, suffered a blinding eye injury during a game in Kitchener. At the height of the public and media outcry, the president of the Canadian Ophthalmological Society (cos), Dr. Page Harshman, asked Dr. Pashby to examine the situation, suggesting that "if there appears to be a problem, Tom, do something about it."

Tom sent a questionnaire to each of the 650 cos members in Canada, requesting their reports of hockey eye injuries treated over the 1972-73 hockey season. A heavy rate of response indicated 287 eye

injuries, including 20 blind eyes. This retrospective study was documented and presented to the 1974 COS annual general meeting in
Edmonton. A prospective study was then recommended and conducted over the 1974-75 hockey season. The results showed 258 eye
injuries and an alarming figure of 43 blind eyes.

With this staggering evidence, immediate action was called for,
and Tom decided that it was high time somebody took on the problem before it became even more catastrophic. It was all very well, he
thought, for players to enjoy the wind in their hair and recklessly display their bravado, for fans to clearly see the faces of their worshipped
players, and for professional marketers to promote the macho character of the game, but if some of this has to be traded off in order for
hockey and its players to survive this terrible epidemic, . . . then so be
it! And Tom was pressed into action.

The major culprit responsible for the 43 blinded eyes in one season of Canadian amateur hockey was mostly hockey stick contact. To
combat this the CAHA introduced new high-sticking rules for the 1975
CAHA rule book. The association also encouraged the production of
eye protection for hockey players. Tom spearheaded a committee for
the Canadian Standards Association (CSA) that was responsible for
writing CSA standards for eye protectors specially designed to prevent

Dr. Tom Pashby enjoys watching his grandson play hockey.
Photo courtesy Dr. Tom Pashby Sports Safety Fund, Toronto, Ontario.

the types of injuries taking place. There were eye protectors on the market, but they allowed a regulation-size hockey stick blade to penetrate the wire mask over each eye and were thus inadequate, indicating that appropriate design and manufacturing standards were needed. As a result of the perseverance and work of Pashby and his committee, by 1977 a preliminary CSA standard was published, and the following year the National Standard of Canada for Face Protectors for Ice Hockey and Box Lacrosse Players was published. In 1979 the CAHA ruled that all minor hockey players must wear a CSA-approved face protector attached to a CSA-approved helmet.

This ruling marked the first such safety standard anywhere, and Pashby's innovative contribution has effectively prevented the extensive suffering and maiming of hockey players throughout the world. Since the establishment of CSA-certification requirements, not one blinding injury has been reported for a minor league player wearing an approved full-face protector, and the average age of injured players has increased dramatically from 14 to 26 because young players have been protected by the new rule.

Meanwhile, according to further reports from the COS, the number of eye injuries suffered by players engaged in other sports, in particular squash and racquetball, prompted immediate attention. And because the eye injuries reported required ophthalmological care, they tended to be severe, 12 percent resulting in a blinded eye. Pashby soon discovered that many of the injuries were incurred by players while they were wearing open eye guards consisting of wire, or open frames, without lenses. Subsequently he and his committee organized and wrote a preliminary CSA standard that was published in 1982, and the inadequate eye guards began to be replaced by polycarbonate lensed protectors. Immediately these improved protectors showed a reduction in eye injuries of no less than 35 percent. The incidence of eye injuries suffered by racquetball and squash players has dropped from 73 percent in 1982, when the COS standard was printed, to 21 percent in 1996.

More eye injuries are incurred by badminton players than by racquetball, squash, and tennis players combined, but new regulations regarding eye protection are coming. Peter Stephenson, vice president, technical, Badminton Canada, reports, "Commencing in September 1997, there will be a three-year staged implementation of protective eyewear starting with the junior age category. We know how difficult it must have been for Dr. Pashby, because even now we are struggling with producing an implementation plan that is acceptable to our membership. In the end, though, we know how worthwhile a project this is, even though it's taken so long to get going, because of Dr. Pashby's inspiration."

Today Dr. Tom Pashby is semiretired and works with his son Bob, who is also an ophthalmologist, and lives with his wife of 56 years in Toronto. His daughter Jane conducts market research in Toronto, while his son Bill is a Toronto lawyer who specializes in corporate law.

4

Fashion Statements

CANADA'S HEAVEN-SCENT CREATION

Michel Germain

After reflecting upon my introductory meeting with Canada's perfume man, Michel Germain, I was amazed by the considerable strength of the initial proposition he developed to establish his creation of séxũal, a sensual and unique fragrance with the potential to be marketed throughout the world. It was then that I realized he had achieved his goal without the benefit of what one would expect to be the most important ingredient: long-term, extensive financial support.

His proposition's great strength lay in his driving belief and commitment to the venture. The personal nature of his rationale in dedicating the concept of séxũal to the love of his life obviously lent enormous power to the marketability of the fragrance that Michel Germain wished to create, especially if one considers that he hadn't actually created it at the time when he enlisted the powers of the industry to assist him and work with him. I also gathered that meticulous attention paid to every detail, however slight, behind the ultra-sensitive theme of séxũal, is fundamental to its success.

Michel is quick to credit a number of individuals for their foresight and willingness to work with him in meeting this formidable challenge. And after meeting him and listening to his interpretation of events leading to his success, I found it easy to understand why he has been able to count on the goodwill and expertise of others. The story of how Germain has become a major world player in the business of scent is a high adventure combining business acumen with creativity and risk taking.

Perfumes are among the most revered international fashion products, and it is nearly impossible for a person to become the creator of a new fragrance without having extraordinary qualifications. Being exorbitantly wealthy certainly helps, having ancestral entitlement is probably expected, and being famous and glamorous is surely a prerequisite at the least. However, even though he doesn't aspire to being a member of any of these categories, Steven Bailey still did it. And "his way" has made a dramatic impact upon the world of high fashion, with its well-established perfume brands such as Calvin Klein, Oscar de la Renta, Yves St. Laurent, Van Cleef & Arpels, and Elizabeth Arden.

Steven Michel Bailey was born in Quebec City in 1964 of bilingual parents, with his mother being French and his father being English. He is the youngest in the family, with one brother, Louis, and three sisters, Patricia, Anne, and Monica. His early education was greatly enhanced by living in a variety of communities throughout eastern Ontario during his father's postings as a member of the Canadian Armed Forces.

Steven received a diploma in electronics engineering technology from Loyalist College in Belleville, Ontario, and he subsequently worked as an engineer for five years. During this period he married Norma Fitzpatrick, and they prepared for the financial independence that they would need in order to pursue the challenging entrepreneurial endeavour they had planned. By saving as much as they could, and even building their own house, Norma and Steven were able to bear the brunt of very little or no income for a few years until their project would generate worthwhile revenue for them. But how much that income would be was impossible to predetermine. The risks were so great that they were almost unthinkable.

Despite his inclination to be a risk taker, Steven is fastidious about details. The concept for his new perfume emanated from what he terms the "manifestation of my creative side," which also called for a more fashionable image, so the paper entity "Michel Germain Parfums Ltd./Ltée." and its Canadian creator, Michel Germain, were born, using a combination of his real middle name, Michel, and Germain, his mother's maiden name. This new identity would also enable the couple to keep their personal lives private, but they soon discovered that their lives were inextricably entwined with Michel Germain Parfums, and they no longer attempt to distance themselves from the company.

"Michel" embarked upon the task of developing a theme based on his adoration of Norma and her aura. He was so utterly captivated by the naturalness of her beauty that he named the fragrance séxūal in her honour. His pretesting of the concept with family and friends by asking them, "How does this concept make you feel?" quickly revealed that it was very appealing, and their enthusiastic response convinced

Michel to investigate the fashion and fragrance industries thoroughly to learn more about women's emotions concerning perfumes. He began to talk to unbiased strangers at department store fragrance and cosmetic counters, on the street, in elevators, and anywhere else where people were willing to comment on his query, "How do you feel about this concept?"

At the same time Michel also sought out business advisers who could give him solid marketing tips and point him to the people whom he would need to blend the oils; create the signature perfume bottle; develop the packaging; design, illustrate, and lay out print materials; write the fashion copy; and otherwise perform the myriad details required just for step one: building the prototypes. After garnering this information, he set out to explore the high-fashion mecca, New York City, where he expected to find one of the "big guys" in the industry who would be enthusiastic about the opportunity to become a partner

with Michel. Although these prospective partners sardonically rolled their eyes at Michel with their "He must be some upstart who came from Canada on a dogsled, because if it's not bottled in New York or from Beverly Hills, forget it" type of attitude, magnanimously (in their own minds) they gave him five minutes of their time and then invariably took an hour. Despite many trips to New York without success in finding a partner, Michel remained objective and as a result could easily tell that he had touched upon the creative nerve centre of these people. Then, while each rejection was still burning within him, he would call a time-out, visit the fragrance counter at Bloomingdale's, and reinstate faith in his concept by discussing it with a person on the frontlines of the business whose opinion he considered good as gold: the perfume saleslady. But by now he knew those in the industry

Norma and Michel Germain, the creator of séxūal perfume.
Photo by Richard Demarais, Demarais Photography Inc., Ottawa, Ontario.

respected his concept enough that they could not dismiss it entirely, so Michel decided to take advantage of all the industrial intelligence that he had been gathering and to do everything himself.

Having identified most of the best artisans and technicians in the industry by this time, Michel knew that the next step was to organize a series of meetings with them. But it wasn't easy; even the initial phone call to each person would take at least three weeks to get through. Mike Sweeney, the senior vice president of new products for International Flavors & Fragrances received Michel's presentation graciously and was so sure of his conviction to forge ahead with Michel that he presented the séxūal concept to 15 of the company's best perfumers. Sophia Grojsman, the world-renowned perfumer whose specialty is this type of project, was designated to handle séxūal. Michel recalls the sparkle in her eye (he always looks for the sparkle in one's eye), and a creative deal was made. séxūal was on the way to realization.

For the signature-bottle design, so important to the emotional appeal of a fragrance, Michel met with the master designer, Pierre Dinand of Paris, whom Michel deemed "such a man of honour, such a gentleman," along with his son Jerome and Pierre's assistant at his showcase offices in the New York City fashion district on 57th Street. Michel discussed his vision in a 35-minute presentation, whereupon Pierre suddenly stood up, shook Michel's hand, and pledged his support for séxūal. Another creative deal was struck, and Pierre applied his considerable prowess to the delivery of Michel's concept. Nothing would stop the magic now, Michel felt.

Developing the fragrance stretched into three years and involved hundreds of renditions in an evolution leading to the final exquisite scent. Work on the creation of the bottle, conducted at the same time, involved tricky hand blowing of prototypes. These faithfully bore the integrity of Pierre's design.

With the finished prototypes in hand, Michel approached Rod Ulmer, vice president of merchandise services for The Bay, having heard of his ability to support new product lines, such as MAC Cosmetics, which he has made successful around the world. Again, after three weeks or so of attempting to get through on the phone, Michel met with Rod, saw that special sparkle in his eye, and landed a contract.

For these three years, the rigorous work involved in manufacturing and all the activities required to bring the product to market were so exhausting that Michel found it difficult to enjoy a complete dinner in a restaurant without having to excuse himself partway through and go to bed. There were four séxūal products in the introductory launch, which meant extra tasks that had to be performed extremely well, because in a new-product launch there is no room for excuses. The extras included hiring and training new staff and stickhandling the Toronto news media at four Toronto branches of The Bay. To this day Michel still doesn't know how he was able to handle everything as he did.

Today, two and a half years later, the entire line of séxūal products, including the men's fragrance, is stocked in The Bay stores, and exports are continually shipped to the Bahamas, Kuwait, Bermuda, Dubai, Hungary, and specialty boutiques in the United States. séxūal now ranks in the top five out of 200 fragrances around the world. Michel believes that anything is achievable provided that one has patience, because good things take time. "It's been seven years. . . . The future is beckoning to us now, and the potential is huge."

Reinventing Nature's Beauty

Thor Grundell

I first learned of the innovative process of turning salmon skin into leather in 1988 when the Canadian government saluted Canadian inventors with an exhibition across the country called Bravo Canada! My invention was chosen along with salmon-skin leather and some 50 other uniquely Canadian inventions, including pablum, the Robertson screwdriver, kerosene, the paint roller, Muskol insect repellant, the walkie-talkie, the goalie mask, and artificial vanilla.

My Bravo Canada! invention was a formula for a pigment to colour live baitfish for sportfishing, and the display received considerable attention from onlookers at the CNE, PNE, and Quebec Expo and was one of the few selected for the Bravo Canada! caravan that travelled for many months to small-town fairs and shopping malls. Since the process of turning salmon skin into leather and dyeing it is related in many ways to my invention, I was naturally drawn by curiosity to investigate what salmon-skin leather was all about.

Even though the information was limited, I found the concept fascinating. And now I have looked into the whole story by speaking with the innovator, Thor Grundell, about his development of salmon-skin leather and the impact of its products in today's marketplace.

On May 7, 1942, Thor Grundell was born in the city of Gothenburg, located at the mouth of the Gota Alv (River) on the west coast of Sweden. His Norwegian mother, Thordis, came from a family of merchants, and his Swedish father, Sven, was a Swedish businessman. Thor's brother Olle was born in 1946. Thor's upbringing included the tang of sea air in his lungs and a primary diet of pickled herring and cod. Not surprising was a penchant in his youth for sportfishing and sailing in summer along the craggy coast, with its rocky shores and fierce ocean weather, and skiing in winter on some of the most rugged ski runs in the world, which was marked in those days by an unspoiled wilderness of towering conifers and massive rock outcroppings to challenge the tough viking spirit of adventure.

Thor attended Commercial College in Gothenburg and the University of Gothenburg, where he studied business economics. In that part of the world, multilingualism is common, but Thor displayed exceptional linguistic talents, being fluent in seven languages. This skill enabled him to excel in the field of import/export marketing, initially with major worldwide steel-fabrication firms.

On February 4, 1974, Thor embarked upon the Canadian leg of his odyssey in business by emigrating to Canada with his wife Nina. They landed on the west coast, and the following September their son was born; they named him Sven in honour of Thor's father. In May 1976 their daughter Lisa was born. At 32 years of age, Thor started afresh at the bottom of the ladder in the steel industry and rose through the ranks until 1981, when he established Grundell International to develop his own import/export business.

As so often happens, it was a childhood memory that inspired and set Thor on his course toward salmon-skin leather. He remembers his mother telling him about her shoes being made of cod skin because of the shortage of animal leathers during World War II. After he came to Canada, he was curious about the possibilities for a fish-skin tannery and the market to go with it. And once he became involved in the challenge, there was no turning back. "My mother told me her cod-skin shoes were tough and lasting, but at that time they didn't know how to treat them properly to get rid of the smell," laughs Thor, "and even today it's especially hard to tan salmon skin. It took our company about five years to get the right finish on the skin before we could go ahead and market it."

Steve Chiu has been the principal tanner for salmon-skin leather since the beginning, and the two innovators formed a joint venture under Grundell International and have recovered after suffering severe losses at the outset. In 1948 Steve was born in Assam, a small country located in northeastern India, of Chinese parents. He worked as a tanner in India in the 1960s and emigrated to Canada in 1976, where he started tanning fish skins for domestic and foreign markets.

Salmon skin was used in early times by the Ingalik Athabaskan Indians to cover babies' cradles because they believed that it had the ability to keep evil spirits away. The Natives also used salmon skin for their babies' coveralls as well as for glorious raingear and other apparel for adults for protection against rain, wind, and uncleanliness.

The Yup'ik people of southwestern Alaska report using fish skins for many generations in the making of mukluks, mittens, and rain-coats. Salmon skin was reserved for special events and people, such as the firstborn child of a chief, if a female, who had to have a hat, muk-luks, and mittens made of female silver salmon skin, while the chief would wear king salmon-skin boots.

Grundell International picks up several million raw salmon skins from fish-processing plants each year to be tanned into leather. Because salmon comprise one of the bigger species caught in great numbers, salmon skins are relatively large and plentiful. Traditionally, this part of the fish is sometimes ground for use as a cheap fertilizer or simply discarded with the rest of the waste material. However, Steve and Thor's innovative concept has created a valuable by-product that makes full use of the resource and provides much-appreciated addi-tional income for fish processors. "Skins were something that was being wasted before. We feel this is a good use of something that would usually be thrown out," Thor says.

According to laboratory tensile strength tests conducted by BASF Canada Incorporated, chum salmon leather is very strong and has the durability of upholstery. Compared to cowhide it is two and a half times stronger. Salmon leather is also scratch resistant and will not shrink like animal leathers because of its marine origin.

There are five species of salmon on the B.C. coast, including chi-nook, coho, pink, chum, and sockeye. Chum salmon is generally the best for tanning and is the least popular variety for sportfishing. The five-step process for making leather takes about 14 days. The skins are first tumbled in a chemical bath and descaled. They are washed repeatedly and placed in a tanning bath, and then they are washed again. Tanning turns the skins white, so they are then dyed, stretched, and dried. Finally a protective and glossy lacquer is added to bring out the natural scale pattern, or a suede finish prized for its ability not to water spot can be produced. With all scales removed prior to tanning, nothing remains on the finished leather to peel or crack.

Thor emphasizes that their salmon-leather products surpass inter-national standards for fine leathers. The development of this technology marks Canada's entry into the high-fashion world of fine exotic leathers. Pink salmon is an especially good type for lapels and cuffs on haute couture jackets and other fashion apparel, including bikinis, which take the product back to its original marine element. The tiny scales on pink salmon give the soft, supple leather an intriguing natural pattern, which has made this leather a very popular fashion-show item. On the other hand, strong chum salmon leather is more appropriate for products requiring great durability.

Salmon leathers are used for making a wide variety of products, including purses, briefcases, wallets, billfolds, belts, buttons, and business card cases. In Japan salmon-leather accordian-pocket business card cases called *meishi* are very popular. In Canada and the United States, manufacturers are buying salmon leathers for making fine-quality shoes and boots, and offshore markets are following suit. High demand for salmon leather comes from the corporate community for use as advertising specialty items, such as key rings and custom designs for all sorts of corporate gifts.

Steve Chiu, his wife, and two sons live in Vancouver. Thor and Nina, his wife of over 25 years, live in West Vancouver, where they are within minutes of sportfishing and sailing in the Pacific Ocean and skiing and hiking in the mountains.

5

Mechanical Wizards

The Legend of Snow Country

Joseph-Armand Bombardier

While I was speaking to Joseph-Armand Bombardier's granddaughter France Bissonnette and listening to her describe her feelings about her phenomenal grandpère, my mind drifted to what it must have been like in the small Quebec town of Valcourt in the 1920s and 1930s when the Bombardier legend began. Quebec hospitality and charm were traditional even then, and the quaint culture wasn't deterred by harsh winters with blowing snow sweeping across the Eastern Townships and blistering summers marked by billowing dust from the roads. For this was the era of the motorized vehicle, and one man provided a uniquely Canadian contribution that has made a tremendous impression around the world. It is indeed a wonderful legacy.

In 1907 Joseph-Armand Bombardier was born in the small Black River Valley town of Valcourt in the Eastern Townships region of Quebec. Even when he was a young boy, Armand astonished his family and friends with his mechanical ability to take old spring clockworks, sewing machines, and motors apart and, using cigar boxes for the bodies, make toy tractors and locomotives that would move on their own. His ability to create impressed his father, Alfred, so much that he allowed Armand to use his farm implement repair tools, just so long as he put them back!

In 1921 his father enrolled Armand in the St. Charles-Baromée seminary in Sherbrooke, Quebec, to study for the priesthood, but it was soon apparent, even to his very disappointed parents, who were hopeful that one of their children would be dedicated to the church, that Armand was destined to pursue his passionate interest in mechanics. He spent more time drawing fantastic machines than studying theology, so despite their desperate urgings, he did not continue at the seminary past his first year.

Armand continually pursued his innovative experiments, and the year that he was 14 he built a cannon out of a discarded shotgun with a broken butt that a friend of his father's gave to him after much pleading. When he returned the weapon a week later to Dr. Archambault, a veterinarian, avid outdoorsman, and gun collector, the cannon was completely modified. Archambault saw how the barrel of his battered old shotgun had been shortened and finished, the firing system rebuilt, and the breech replaced. Young Armand had also sawn and polished the butt and turned out two wooden wheels on his father's lathe and attached them. Armand loaded the cannon and fired it, much to Archambault's alarm, and the doctor made Armand promise never to fire the weapon again because it was very dangerous. However, he was very excited to witness this demonstration of Armand's extraordinary faculty for engineering, and he spread the word even further about this promising young talent.

After Armand left the seminary for summer holidays, he had his first experience with steam power. He assembled a boiler, tubes, valves, a piston and a drive shaft, added some old sewing machine parts, managed to get an old tire pump, and began to build a machine. Enlisting the help of his aunt Marie, he convinced her to let him use her valued spinning wheel and attached it to an inflated inner tube. After testing the machine and seeing the spinning wheel move, Armand carried the works over to the church, where some boiler mechanics were repairing the heating system. Curious about Armand's machine, they promised him that they would test it the next day. After a sleepless night for the young inventor, as promised they hooked it up to the steam pipes, and the marvellous machine worked, but in minutes it blew apart from the pressure of the steam. Armand's first contact with steam power was a qualified success, so later that year his father decided to buy him a worn-out Ford to tinker with.

With his like-minded younger brother Léopold, Armand set to work on the old motor during their Christmas holidays. Within weeks they had built a vehicle with a wooden propeller and mounted upon four runners from a horse-drawn sleigh. On January 31, 1922, the vehicle was taken out onto the streets of Valcourt, and amid bolting horses and barking dogs, the infernally noisy contraption trundled up the street for a kilometre with furious townsfolk, in particular their Papa, shouting at them to shut it down. It was terribly noisy and extremely dangerous, but it worked! So, at only 15 years of age, testing his first snowmobile pro- totype in public, Joseph-Armand Bombardier began a lifelong infatua- tion with the concept for a vehicle to travel on snow that would eventually develop into a highly popular outdoor winter sport and a major worldwide industry, with his company as the undisputed leader.

In 1924 Armand landed his first job as a mechanic's apprentice at a small auto repair shop in the nearby town of South Stukely. He contin- ued his studies of electrical engineering and mechanics, steadfastly keeping in mind his vision of creating a vehicle that could travel effi- ciently on snow to relieve snowbound people from being completely isolated during winter because it was impossible to drive cars in the Quebec countryside. However, he despaired from the lack of immedi- ate potential that the small town of Valcourt appeared to hold for him, so he packed his bags one summer day and set out for Montreal, where he expected that opportunities awaited. He was then all of 17.

Life in the big city, as Armand soon discovered, was not a piece of cake. He found lodging with an aunt and uncle and immediately regis- tered for evening courses in mechanics and electrical engineering sponsored by the Ford Motor Company. He was able to avoid the temp- tations of Montreal in the 1920s and spent all his savings on technical books, after which he took a menial job in a garage until finally he demonstrated his uncanny ability at a much larger auto repair garage and landed a job there as a mechanic, first-class.

Two years later Armand had acquired the good theoretical and practical training that he needed and headed back to his hometown to start up his own business. In April 1926 his father bought some land upon which he could build a garage for his son, who'd just turned 19. That summer Armand opened Garage Bombardier, became a dealer for Imperial Oil, and fixed cars and every other type of machine from sawmills and threshers to ice saws and pumps. He was in his glory. He thrived on diagnosing difficult problems and resolving them quickly. Soon his reputation was widely known, and he could not cope with the flow of business. His uncle Aurélien joined him, then his brother Léopold came in, then a future brother-in-law, Valmore Labrecque, and a raft of other mechanically inclined family members and friends jumped on board the Garage Bombardier bandwagon.

Armand's inventiveness was the fuel that ran the business. He built the equipment that he needed with his own hands and depended on no one. He once forged a drill and hydraulic press for producing steel and cast iron cylinders, gas tanks, and heaters. In 1930 he even built his own dam and turbine on the stream alongside his garage to harness energy for his own use years before the town of Valcourt brought in electricity.

On August 7, 1929, Armand married Yvonne, the love of his life, and they began to raise their family. Times got tough as the Great Depression settled in, but Garage Bombardier survived, and Armand was determined to replace Quebec's only mode of winter travel, horse-drawn sleds, with a motorized vehicle. Through 10 long winters from 1926 to 1936, Armand wrestled with the many problems of designing a machine to travel over snow, with its changing densities and unique sit-uations. He identified three areas of concern. First, the vehicle's weight needed to be evenly distributed to keep the machine level. Second, he needed a suitable propulsion system that was safe and reliable and could be cooled. Third, the vehicle needed to have suspension that afforded passengers a comfortable ride.

During this period Armand faced abject failures and stood up to subsequent criticism from many cynics. He weathered the storm, but when tragedy struck it was a bitter blow. One night their two-year-old son Yvon needed immediate hospital treatment for appendicitis and peritonitis, but the nearest hospital was about 50 kilometres distant in Sherbrooke, and the roads were snowed in. While an unfinished snow-mobile languished in Armand's garage, young Yvon died, just like oth-ers who also weren't able to reach a doctor during winter. Armand's resolve to create a machine that would relieve them from such hazards of winter became even more determined. He gave up trying to develop a smaller, lighter vehicle and instead set out to design a larger vehicle that could carry several passengers.

In the following year, 1936, he invented the B7, which stood for Bombardier and the number of passengers that it could carry in its light plywood cabin. It marked the end of a 10-year quest. He applied for a patent on 21 December 1936, and it was granted on 29 June 1937. By then Armand had already begun production of eight orders, which sub-sidized the building of more than 25 vehicles the following year. By this time Armand had closed the automobile repair shop and erected a new sign over the doors of the garage – "L'Auto-Neige Bombardier" – and it signalled the beginning of a new Bombardier era. The company flourished until the outbreak of World War II, when Bombardier began to assist the war effort to the extent that the firm was almost rendered insolvent. Armand was contracted by the Canadian army to supply snowmobiles for military purposes, but because the demand was immediate and required special models that would keep him busy designing, he was forced to subcontract most of the business out to assorted vehicle-parts manufacturers in Quebec. These firms were thus built up and collectively established what has become a major industry in the province of Quebec today.

During the war years and the years following, many superb models of Bombardier snowmobiles were designed and built, new plants were constructed, and more people were hired to accommodate the burgeoning business. By the end of the 1940s, Armand was still working on multiple-passenger vehicles, although he deplored their use by single travellers such as doctors, missionaries, trappers, and prospectors, all of whom travelled alone. He reasoned that the market needed a small snowmobile, but the obstacles were very involved and required substantial financial resources in order to mount redesign and manufacturing. However, in 10 years he was able to overcome the obstacles, and finally, in early 1959, local residents heard the unmistakable roar of

One of the first snowmobiles, a 1936 model B7, in front of Armand's shop which was built for him in 1926. Photo courtesy Musée J. Armand Bombardier, Valcourt, Quebec.

Armand and his men zooming through the countryside on their new lightweight snowmobile. It was called a Ski-Dog. When the literature for the Ski-Dog was printed, a typographical error changed the name to Ski-Doo, and Armand's innovative sense told him to go with it, so the name Ski-Doo stuck.

The Ski-Doo was introduced in 1959 and was an instant hit. Each year the vehicle and the sport grew immensely in popularity. In the February 1963 issue of *Imperial Oil Review,* Bill Stephenson wrote that "this kind of scooter mounted on toy tracks and which growls like a runaway dishwasher" became highly sought after everywhere.

Joseph-Armand Bombardier passed away on February 18, 1964. During his lifetime he was granted more than 40 patents, and the J. Armand Bombardier Museum in Valcourt, Quebec, provides a permanent home for his inventions.

Today Bombardier Incorporated is a world-leading company engaged in systems design and manufacturing for the aerospace industry, transportation equipment, motorized consumer products, and their supporting capital and services requirements. Armand would be proud.

Making the
Airways Safer

Jerry Wright

Before Jerry Wright invented the R-Theta computer in 1950, the tech-niques that were necessary to enable a navigator to plot an accurate return course home were extremely involved. Even under the best of conditions, it was an unwieldy and not entirely reliable system. Navigators had to consider dead reckoning with latitude and longitude, true headings, drift-sighting, rhumb lines, celestial bearings, weather almanacs and visible indicators for estimated changes, charts, and ulti-mately gut feelings. For a navigator to be intimately familiar with all the complex components of the procedure, it took years of training and continual experience in the field with all of the myriad situations that could develop. But despite all this intelligence, the system still was far from being foolproof, and air navigators were faced with knowing that even the slightest miscalculation could result in tragic consequences.

However, when the R-Theta computer came on the scene, for the first time, fighter aircraft pilots in particular could rely upon being able to return home safely, and the innovation is credited with saving innu-merable lives until the R-Theta was finally replaced in the 1970s by super-high-precision gyroscopic technology, which persisted until satel-lite navigation systems came along. The R-Theta computer also guided fighter pilots to their mission destination if it was a moving target such as an enemy bomber. In order to home-in on the target, one-on-one ground control was necessary to direct the fighter, and when the enemy jammed radio communications, instead of being cast adrift, the R-Theta took over and enabled the fighter pilot to complete the mission independently.

Because Wing Commander J.G. Wright was a member of the Canadian Armed Forces when he invented the R-Theta system, the Canadian government held all proprietary rights to the invention and earned royalties in excess of $1 million from only one of a number of private manufacturers of the product.

With his R-Theta computer and many other inventions, Wright's selfless contribution to air travel throughout the world as well as to Canadian society as a whole is a superb example of Canadian ingenuity and patriotism. His story is fascinating and unique in the annals of Canadian inventors.

Jerauld George Wright was born in Nova Scotia on August 31, 1917, in a town named after Liverpool, England, complete with the Mersey River alongside. Jerry fondly remembers his youth there. The Wright family home was on the same lot as his grandfather's house, and Jerry spent much of his spare time there with his grandpa, learning how to use his carpentry tools and the wide range of construction materials fastidiously collected and stored there over the years. This early exposure kindled the budding young inventor's interests as a designer and builder, and at an early age he was building ice craft with his friends and cruising up and down the Mersey River during the winter. As a professional carpenter, his grandpa constructed large wooden master containers for coffins on contract, and Jerry made good use of the many extras that were always available, including using them as risers for stages when he and his friends put on performances and for other things that they continually built and

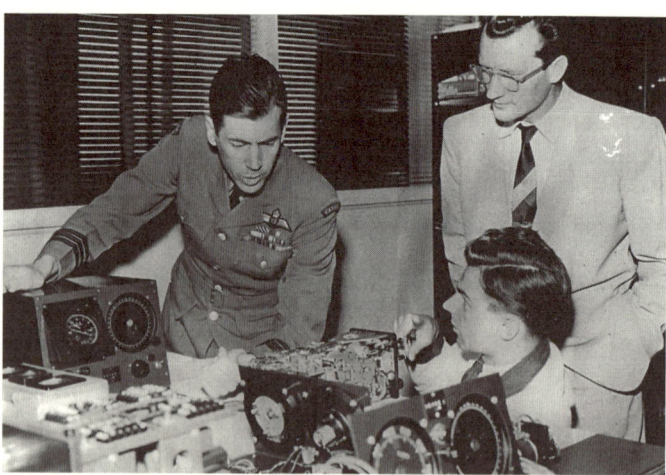

The R-Theta Navigation Computer System disassembled in centre. From left to right are inventor Wing Commander J.G. Wright; J.M. Monty Bridgman, President of Photographic Survey Corp. (now Spar Aerospace) of Toronto, Ontario; and Karl Papp.

tore down to satisfy their fleeting childhood whims.

In 1934 Jerry completed high school at 16 years of age. Since money was scarce in those days, his parents couldn't afford full-time university tuition for him, so he took a certification course at university qualifying him for a job as a pharmaceutical clerk. He worked at a Liverpool drugstore until 1940, shortly after World War II broke out, when he was lured to join the Royal Canadian Air Force as an AC 2 trainee navigator, the lowest possible rank in the service.

Following enlistment, Jerry spent several weeks in general indoctrination, including armament drills, then rose to the rank of corporal, took a celestial-navigation training course at Canadian Forces Base Trenton, Ontario, became a sergeant, and was shipped overseas on December 15. He arrived in Greenock, Scotland, on Christmas Day 1940 with his buddies, ready to win the war.

But they weren't needed, and since they weren't allowed to stay in their barracks after breakfast, they had nothing else to do but wander around town all day. Finally their orders came through, and Jerry was given a hasty three-week training stint and assigned to be the navigator on a Stranraer flying boat, whose mission was to conduct submarine patrols in the North Sea. These flying boats could endure six to eight hours in flight, but the next year he was assigned to a Catalina flying boat which had an increased range of 18 to 20 hours on regular patrols or 32 hours by being equipped with overload tanks. Navigation techniques were basic, relying on celestial bearings, if the stars were visible, or on dead reckoning, which simply involved mapping with a protractor. Many of these missions were flown for a whole day over the open ocean with no landmarks to give a reading, but by watching the wave action and whitecaps, a good navigator could estimate airspeed compensation if clouds or fog didn't obscure the ocean surface. Using a drift-sight to measure drift angles, gauge wind velocity, and provide offsets from compass directions was the customary navigational procedure. The navigator became a good bluffer with experience, and Jerry laughingly recalls using "iffy" weather-forecasting terms so well that the pilot would often be seen shaking his head in amazement after landing exactly at the estimated time of arrival. "We've got the best nav on the map," the pilot would crow.

Throughout the years of navigating during patrols for enemy submarines along the coast of northern Europe, Jerry had the opportunity of working with virtually all the different navigation equipment available and using all the latest techniques being developed. He worked with many other navigators, and he contributed his accumulating knowledge to updating celestial manuals and charts to develop their four-year-interval almanacs.

On his reassignment during 1942-44, as navigation officer of 240 Squadron, RAF, based at Madras, India, Jerry devised a celestial-navigation formula using the sun, moon, and stars to get a fix on a destination. During this time he also developed a more compact guide by using three instead of four configurations, and his almanac was heralded by the highest RAF navigation authorities, and he was promoted to flight lieutenant. The missions at that time involved dropping spies into Burma, and safety requirements were high, necessitating precise timing and location for each drop.

During 1944-45 Jerry became part of a braintrust group of nine at Shawbury, England, who concentrated upon the study of all navigational systems developed in private industry and military service up to that time. It was then that Jerry focused all of his intense navigational experience upon developing some way to make a pilot aware of where he was in relation to home base. As a result of the stimulating working milieu in Shawbury, Jerry conceived the dynamics of the R-Theta computer and proceeded to design a machine that would fit into the tiny area available in a fighter, provide an instantaneous reading so that a pilot could concentrate on other priorities, and display the reading continuously so that the pilot always knew the direction of home and how far it was. For pilots this machine was an exceptional benefit in any war or peacetime flight. The name R-Theta is a combination of trigonometry terms in which "R" stands for range and "Theta" means angle.

At the time of this writing, Wing Commander J.G. Wright is retired and living in Gloucester, Ontario, with his wife Margaret Elizabeth, whom he married in 1942. Daughters Christine and Alison, and sons Ian and Robert, are grown and are raising their own families, perhaps in the spirit of their intrepid and inventive father, who watches for the signs of inventiveness in some of his grandchildren. In the meantime, Wright is not completely satisfied with his many achievements, including holding patents for some 30 inventions, including a ground speed and interception computer, an air navigation and tactical control system, a great circle computer, an integrated direction indicator, a master direction indicator, a tactical display system, a Doppler-coupled navigation system, a star-coupled direction corrector, a circle projector for anti-sub activities, a handheld navigation computer, a track plotter, and house building systems. He is also co-inventor of the Position Homing Indicator. He currently leases out rights to the patented automatic self-propelled swimming pool cleaner and his latest innovation, a patented modular residential construction system.

Turning Up the Heat

Thomas Ahearn

The modest beginnings of Thomas Ahearn as part of a large Irish immigrant family didn't deter him from building a number of major businesses that, with his considerable knack and foresight, fostered his many inventions. His great vision and courage are epitomized by his invention of the electric stove, an incredible feat when one realizes that it was the first time that anything other than fire was used for cooking food. Ahearn had that spark of innovative audacity to sell many ideas that would profoundly improve the lives of Canadians of his time. I can't imagine how he was able to convince the civic leaders of Ottawa to approve the stringing up of exposed electrical cables on the main thoroughfares of the national capital city to power streetcars for public transportation.

The list of his outstanding achievements is considerable. Ahearn was a pioneer developer of hydroelectric power, and he invented a number of electrical appliances, including water heaters and audio-reproduction devices. And after a dazzling career in private business, this amazing man became a noted public servant of national consequence.

Thomas Ahearn was born in 1855 in Le Breton Flats, the lumber district of Ottawa, in a large house on Ashburnham Hill. As he grew up, he had neither wealthy nor influential friends, but he was endowed with a zest for innovation and the manual dexterity to go with it.

After leaving Ottawa College (now the University of Ottawa) and still in his teens, Thomas landed his first job with the Montreal Telegraph Company at no pay in return for learning telegraphy and worked at its Chaudière office on the premises of J.R. Booth, the lumber king. He learned to be a telegrapher within a year, and at 18 he joined Western Union Telegraph in New York City. He returned to

Ottawa two years later as chief operator for the Montreal Telegraph Company.

In 1879 his youthful exuberance led to a momentous event in the development of the telephone: he established a successful connection for the 110 miles between Ottawa and Pembroke. Having copied Alexander Graham Bell's invention of the telephone from an article in *Scientific American*, young Ahearn fashioned two sets using cigar boxes, but he wasn't aware that he had actually infringed upon Bell's patent, for he'd simply wanted to be able to talk with a fellow telegraph operator in Pembroke. To settle a hotel bill later on, he sold his homemade cigar-box telephones for $16.

Following the incorporation of Bell Telephone in 1880, Ahearn was hired to manage Bell's Ottawa office, likely because his celebrated transgression of Bell's invention only a year before had focused attention on his ability. For young Ahearn changes were happening quickly. In 1881 he and American Warren Soper, Ottawa office manager of Dominion Telegraph, recognized enormous potential in the field of electricity, resigned their positions, and formed a partnership named Ahearn and Soper, Electrical Contractors. As Ottawa-district representatives of the Westinghouse Electric Manufacturing Company of Chicago, they persuaded George Westinghouse to build an electrical appliance manufacturing plant in Hamilton.

In 1870 Ottawa's public transportation consisted of six small horse-drawn streetcars; to keep passengers warm in winter, the floors were covered with straw and the cars were heated with a tiny coal stove. In February 1888 the electric street railway made a hit with the people of Richmond, Virginia, but the system was not considered viable for Ottawa because of winter conditions. A delegation of U.S. interests attempted to secure a contract with Ottawa, but negotiations eventually fell through, to the glee of cynics. However, Ahearn was able to convince the city to allow Ahearn and Soper to form a local company to construct and operate the street railway in Ottawa. Local financiers proved difficult because they did not believe that the project was feasible, but when Ahearn and Soper finally won the contract, the Ottawa Electric Railway was established in 1891 with Ahearn as president, and Soper as vice president.

The first small electric cars for public transit appeared on Ottawa streets eight months later. To manufacture the streetcars, Ahearn and

Soper also formed the Ottawa Car Company from what had been the Wylie Carriage factory. Ahearn invented and patented efficient electric heaters, and the streetcars were supplied to 12 major cities across Canada. Also, to keep the track clear in winter, he invented a rotating brush cleaner. Ottawa Electric Railway was privately run for 58 years; it was taken over by the city in 1948 and eventually became O-C Transpo, the company responsible for public transit in Ottawa today.

The sumptuous Russell House in the centre of the city, called the political headquarters of the Dominion, was the site for another Ahearn innovation: the installation of an electric motor to power the hotel's freight elevator. His most public achievement was heralded by a splendid event at the Ottawa Windsor Hotel dining room on August 29, 1892, to celebrate his invention of and patents for cooking heaters, as these first electric stoves were called. The hotel menu was imprinted with this proud declaration:

Every item on this menu has been cooked by the electric heating appliance invented and patented by Mr. T. Ahearn of Ahearn and Soper of this City and is the first instance in the history of the world of an entire meal being cooked by electricity. The bread and meats were cooked in an electric oven and the liquids in other electric heaters.

Electric Dinner

SOUP

Consommé Royal

FISH

Saginaw Trout With Potato Croquetts, Cream Tartar

BOILED

Sugar Cured Ham, Champagne Sauce
Spring Chicken With Parsley Sauce
Beef Tongue Sauce Piquant

ROAST

Sirloin Of Beef And Horse Radish
Turkey With Cranberry Sauce
Stuffed Loin Of Veal, Lemon Sauce

ENTRÉES

Larded Sweetbreads With Mushrooms
Lamb Cutlets And Green Peas
Strawberry Puffs

VEGETABLES

Potatoes, Plain And Mashed, Cream Corn, Escalloped
Tomatoes, Vegetable Marrow

PUDDING AND PASTRY

Apple Soufflés, Wine Sauce, Apple Pie, Black Currant Tart, Chocolate Cake,
Coconut Drops, Vanilla Ice Cream, Marachino Jelly

FRUITS

Apples, Raisins, English Walnuts, Almonds, Watermelon, Grapes
Black Tea, Green Tea, Coffee, Cheese, Biscuits

The *Ottawa Journal* of August 29, 1892, featured "the first meal cooked by electricity" as "cooking by the agency of chained lightning." Ahearn traded his patent rights to the American Heating Corporation in return for stock, but unfortunately the company went bankrupt before he was able to make any money with his sensational invention.

In 1885 Ahearn's firm, the Ottawa Electric Light Company, was contracted to install 165 arc street lamps, the first time that electricity was used for light in the city. To accommodate the contract, the company first built a very simple power station driven by a water wheel and was able to upgrade the system within a short period to provide a citywide electrical service. In 1887 Ahearn formed the Chaudière Electric Company across the river in Hull, Quebec, bought out the Standard Electric Company competition, and secured a monopoly on providing electric power to the city. As the renowned standard for hydroelectric systems throughout Canada, the Ottawa Electric Company showed other municipalities how they too could conquer the extensive difficulties of hydroelectric operation. The hydroelectric company that Ahearn developed is now known as Ottawa Hydro, and since he also invented the electric water heater, Ottawa Hydro still rents these appliances as part of its services. He also built telegraph lines that later became the North American Telegraph System.

This electric sweeper which kept streetcar tracks free of snow and ice in winter was among Thomas Ahearn's many inventions. Photo courtesy Lilias Ahearn.

In the *Ottawa Citizen* of September 12, 1899, Ahearn's trend-setting style of driving the first electric automobile in Ottawa was noted:

> *The first Automobile or horseless carriage was seen on the streets of Ottawa yesterday morning. Mr. Thomas Ahearn who has the distinction of being the first to use the carriage, was in charge and manipulated it with apparent ease. The speed of the carriage can be varied from two to fifteen miles per hour and the motor is furnished by electricity. The motion is silent but swift. It is expected that a number of these carriages will be on exhibition at the next Fair.*

For the 1927 celebration of the Diamond Jubilee of Confederation, Ahearn was appointed by Prime Minister William Lyon Mackenzie King to the position of chairman of the Broadcasting Committee to organize his innovative concept – the special events on Parliament Hill programmed on the country's first coast-to-coast radio broadcast, a formidable challenge in those days considering that radio was in its infancy. A vast network of some 20,000 miles of wire to connect British Columbia through the Rocky Mountains and across the Prairies to northern Ontario, Quebec, and Moncton, over which no voice had ever spoken before, was an overwhelming feat, but Ahearn was known to rise to the most difficult of innovative challenges. In appreciation of his organization of this historic broadcast, he was sworn in as privy councillor on January 10, 1928, and given the title Honourable with the right to use the abbreviation PC after his name.

By beautifying the national capital, Ahearn contributed further in public service as chairman of the Ottawa Improvement Commission, which is now the National Capital Commission, and even financed the construction of one of the region's major bridges across the Ottawa River, the Champlain Bridge, from his own pocket.

The Honourable Thomas Ahearn, PC, patented 11 Canadian inventions from 1891 to 1921: checks for commodities measured by meters, electric flat iron, electric heater, electric oven, electric warming bottle, method of heating an automatic water supply electrically, system of warming cars by means of electrically heated water, sound-reproducing mechanisms, talking machine, and sound machinery. He was the president of nine major firms and utilities and the vice president of a realty company, held six directorships, and was chairman of two key public offices. Ahearn was indeed an outstanding innovative Canadian, and his service to his country as well as his city is legendary.

6

The Mighty Communicators

Canada's Great Forgotten Inventor

Reginald Fessenden

On September 28, 1901, Reginald Aubrey Fessenden, born in Quebec and raised and educated in southern Ontario, patented the heterodyne principle, which is fundamental to all radio, including the many modes of telecommunication today. He coined the term "heterodyne" from the Greek words heteros, meaning "other" or "different," and dynamis, meaning "power." On December 12, 1901, an Italian by the name of Guglielmo Marconi conducted his famous trans-Atlantic experiment in which he said that he heard a Morse code transmission of the letter s, which is three short clicks (did-did-did), on Signal Hill in St. John's, Newfoundland, that was a one-way wireless telegraphy from a sender located in Poldhu, Cornwall, England. But Fessenden had earlier sent voice over radio, wireless telephony in 1900.

In spite of his early important and numerous inventions and accomplishments, Fessenden never received the support of his fellow Canadians. Only Marconi received the blessing of the Canadian government, including a grant and licensing commitments, forcing Fessenden to continue with his experiments and inventions south of the border, where a new firm, the National Electric Signalling Company, was founded to market his inventions. However, RCA (Radio Company of America) acquired Fessenden's patents from NESC and squelched them (until the late 1920s). In 1928 Fessenden was awarded a $500,000 out-of-court settlement from RCA, finally vindicating and financially rewarding him, even though it was very late in his life.

Marconi is still mistakenly called the Father of Radio, but bits of information here and there almost set the record straight for Fessenden. Yet the credits that Fessenden receives are often qualified by statements that he was a poor businessman, an angry genius ignored by his own country, or a red-bearded burly man with a huge temper who frightened people. But I hope that we can now put an end to this commentary and properly recognize this brilliant inventor for his fabulous contributions to our society. The following profile is dedicated to the memory of Reginald A. Fessenden in gratitude for the hundreds of his inventions, mostly in the field of telecommunications, that have added so much colour and comfort to our lives.

On October 6, 1866, Reginald Aubrey Fessenden was born in the village of East Bolton in Quebec's Eastern Townships region. His mother was named Clementina, his father was a minister by the name of Elisha, and he had three younger brothers. His maternal grandfather, Edward Trenholme, had been an innovator of some distinction, having invented the grain elevator and a snowplow for railroads, among other things. His uncle, Cortez Fessenden, was a math and physics teacher, and he greatly influenced young Reginald's interests in science and inventing, having introduced him to *Scientific American* magazine, the fine publication still issued today.

In 1874 the family moved to Fergus, Ontario, where Reginald began to avidly pursue his inventiveness, building a small wooden model of a snowplow powered by an engine constructed from parts that he salvaged from an old clock. Shortly after, the family moved again, this time to the town of Suspension Bridge, near Niagara Falls.

Reginald received a scholarship from De Veaux Military College across the bridge in New York state and excelled in his schoolwork interspersed with military drills. After a year at De Veaux, he left for the famous Canadian boarding school, Trinity College School, in Port Hope, Ontario, and did very well there, during one year winning all the prizes in his class.

By the time that Reginald was 14, he required surgery to correct a growing problem with his eyes, and despite lost school time for his recuperation, he still graduated from Trinity at only 15 years of age. The next year he became a math teacher at Bishop's College in Lennoxville, Quebec, and worked toward a degree at the same time. When he was 17 he was named principal of the Whitney Institute on the Island of Bermuda, and there he met his bride-to-be, Helen May Trott. After a two-year stint at the institute, Reginald left Bermuda for New York to work for the renowned inventor, Thomas Edison. For Edison he invented a safe electrical-wire covering, a new type of varnish, an electrical gyroscope for land, water, and air navigation, and a wide variety of other things. Thus began a fabulous career during which he would become one of the world's most prolific inventors.

Unfortunately in 1890 the Edison companies floundered. Reginald and Helen were married even though he was laid off, but he immediately landed another job, this time with George Westinghouse. Working for Westinghouse, Reginald invented a better lightbulb than the Edison version and worked on the design of electric generators and other machinery, but that business also ran into financial woes, and in 1892 he was back on the street again. After all this experience, he was by now only 26.

Of necessity Reginald returned to teaching, landing a job at Purdue University in Lafayette, Indiana, where his son Ken was born, and the next year he became professor of electrical engineering at the University of Pittsburgh. Reginald was then appointed to a new engineering position at Western University in Allegheny, Pennsylvania, which located him closer to Westinghouse's factory, where he was able to conduct some consulting work in his spare time.

Meanwhile, in 1895, news from Italy described how a young innovator, Guglielmo Marconi, had successfully invented the wireless transmission of telegraphy over a long distance, and this invention could be of great value to the navigation of ships by keeping them in contact with shore and each other. Industry and governments greeted this news with keen interest. This information galvanized Reginald to design a whole new system of wireless transmission. Telephony had made some of the telegraphic business obsolete, so he concluded that wireless telephony could very well make wireless telegraphy obsolete. And because wireless telephony was not possible with Marconi's system, Reginald concentrated on

Reginald Aubrey Fessenden portrait from Radio's First Voice *by Ormond Raby.*
Photo courtesy Communications Research Centre, Ottawa, Ontario.

wireless telephony. His early work was dominated by his interest in transmitting words without wires, but since the news of Marconi's attempts to achieve trans-Atlantic communication caught the attention of the world, Fessenden turned his attention to wireless telegraphy; he was convinced that his method of using continuous waves was far superior for wireless telegraphy (necessary for wireless telephony) than the Marconi system.

In 1900 Fessenden built his own wireless telegraph, and that spring he took a job with the U.S. Weather Bureau conducting research into wireless telegraphy on Cobb Island in the Potomac River, located 100 kilometres from Washington, D.C. After building the first wireless station in North America at Cobb Island, Reginald sent messages – with the help of Alfred Thiessen – between two 15-metre-high telegraph masts located a kilometre apart and another tower about 80 kilometres distant. Since the Weather Bureau was interested only in Morse code telegraphic messages, Reginald worked on transmitting voice messages with wireless telephony on his own time.

On December 23, 1900, instead of sending a message in Morse code across Cobb Island to Thiessen, Reginald succeeded in transmitting these historic words over wireless telephony, "One, two, three, four. Is it snowing where you are, Mr. Thiessen? If it is, telegraph back and let me know." Thiessen confirmed the message immediately, and the world's first spoken radio message had been sent by the inventor, Reginald A. Fessenden.

Following constant improvements to his wireless system, in 1901 Reginald was able to transmit wireless telephony over a distance of 60 miles to Cape Hatteras across Pamlico Sound. The Fessendens and Thiessen organized a new Weather Bureau site on Roanoke Island off the North Carolina coast. Fessenden kept developing his wireless telegraphy for the Weather Bureau, sending messages farther and farther. He also kept up the pace with his radio, sending his voice and music over 100 kilometres. Then the Weather Bureau demanded 50 percent proprietary rights to his inventions, and when Reginald refused he was fired. The year was 1902, and our intrepid inventor was on the street again, still trying to finance his wireless telephony.

Fessenden then applied to the Canadian government for funding but was turned down because the government had followed the

British and backed Marconi, granting him government money and exclusive rights to erect towers on Canada's east coast, even though his system was definitely inferior. So Fessenden sought out two millionaire investors from Pittsburgh, and they capitalized the National Electric Signalling Company, installing Fessenden as manager with the job of building and operating telegraph stations in order to charge customers for sending messages. Later on the company intended to market Reginald's wireless telephony system. In launching their company, they drew attention to trans-Atlantic telegraph capabilities, so they built two extra stations with masts 120 metres tall, one at Brant Rock, Massachusetts, and the other at Machrihanish, Scotland. In January 1906 both stations were in full wireless telegraphic operation, and Fessenden had pulled ahead of Marconi.

With his radio developments, Fessenden conducted various experiments, sending the day's fish prices to a fishing boat and sending messages about 17 kilometres between Brant Rock and Plymouth. Later that year he discovered that one of his voice messages from Brant Rock to Plymouth had been received by the station in Scotland. He had sent a wireless telephony message across the Atlantic with ease.

By the end of 1906, Fessenden was ready to demonstrate the world's first radio broadcast, a Christmas concert for sailors on the United Fruit Company's banana boats bound for U.S. markets. He gave a speech, played a recording of Handel's Largo, performed a solo on his violin, and extended season's greetings. Then he broadcast another performance on New Year's Eve.

Fessenden kept inventing despite flagrant violations of his patents and expensive legal battles. After the sinking of the Titanic in 1912, he invented the radio sonar to avert future tragedies. Later that year he built a machine for the Submarine Signal Company that could send wireless messages 80 kilometres under water. During World War I, he invented improved gun sights, devices to detect German zeppelins and submarines, and other major life-saving gadgets. In 1921 he left the Submarine Signal Company, and on January 14, 1927, he filed a U.S. patent for a television apparatus. His wife, Helen, also filed a follow-on patent on November 3, 1936, after Reginald's death.

Finally, in 1928, Fessenden received a reported $500,000 in an out-of-court settlement from RCA for patent violations, but by then heart troubles forced him into retirement. In his house in Bermuda on July 22, 1932, he passed away with 500 patents to his name, leaving the world a much better place for his having been here. The *New York Herald Tribune* wrote, "It sometimes happens, even in science, that one man can be right against the world. Professor Fessenden was that man."

TUNING OUT BAD TV

Tim Collings

Soon after television was introduced, many parents allowed their children to be taken over and almost raised by it. When the weather was unpleasant for playing outdoors, when mom and dad longed for peace and quiet, television was the undisputed entertainer of the kids, who behaved themselves and learned a lot about the world. In that respect things don't appear to have changed much in almost 50 years.

But for a long time, television programs seem to have become intently focused upon drawing the attention of larger audiences, and subsequently the highest possible advertising rates. The integrity of programming aimed at or seen by people with impressionable minds, particularly children, has been lost. During the last few years, many people have spoken out against offensive television programs; they believe that profanity, violence, and pornography on TV promote dangerous behaviour in a segment of society that is extremely vulnerable.

But nothing has satisfactorily addressed the growing problem, made even more complex by cable television. Finally, though, one man has taken the initiative to create a device that helps people to keep objectionable programming out of their homes. The recent invention of the V-Chip by Tim Collings has given the world an easy and inexpensive solution to this major problem, and in so doing he may have saved television from itself. I hope so, because television, despite its defects, is still a great babysitter and a wonderful source of information, especially for children.

Tim Collings was born on September 2, 1961, in London, Ontario, and was the second child for Jacqueline and Thomas Collings. When Tim was two years old, the Collings moved to a farm near Stratford. A civil engineer, Thomas worked for the county. The family welcomed three more boys and two more girls and settled into a robust life on the farm raising beef cattle, sheep, and chickens, as well as growing hay and field corn to feed the stock.

In retrospect Tim considers that his life on the farm built his resourcefulness: "If your tractor broke down in the middle of a field somewhere, you'd have to know how to fix it on the spot because you needed it to get back home." He particularly enjoyed haying and working with the farm machinery. And he relished the wonderful days of his youth in the country, growing up with the Avon River and two ponds nearby for swimming in summer and skating and hockey in winter.

Tim attended Downie Central, a country school nearby, and graduated in 1979 from Stratford Central Secondary High School. He graduated in 1984 with his bachelor of applied science in electrical engineering degree and received his master of applied science in electrical control systems degree in 1986, both from the University of Waterloo.

His first job was developing products for SAF Drive Systems, a major manufacturer of electric drives for AC and DC motors. This job gave Tim hands-on experience for his master's thesis. He wanted to upgrade older analog-based drive systems with microprocessor-based technology. As a consultant for SAF Drive Systems, he travelled throughout North America investigating engineering systems applications in various environments, including pulp and paper mills, steel mills, and any others requiring a motor to drive materials.

On his development of the V-Chip, Tim recalls the sequence of events, beginning with the first glimmer of the concept: "My journey began on December 6, 1989. I was thousands of miles away in my office at Simon Fraser University listening to a CBC news bulletin reporting that a gunman had walked into École Polytechnique in Montreal and shot fourteen women. At the time no one really knew how many would die. After hearing the news of the massacre, I headed home and, in my living room with my wife among the cheerful Christmas decorations, I watched the horrifying news unfold on television. It was just days from the Christmas semester break.

"Canada was in shock. In the face of such a great loss, there was a search for meaningful fundamental truths, an explanation. In the aftermath of the tragedy, a number of reports referred to Marc

Lepine's steady diet of violent videos; in that context there were many references to several studies about how television affects us. The question presenting itself to me was this: could Lepine's militant, psychotic misogyny somehow have been manifested in these ultraviolent acts as a result of his exposure to recurring media images of glamourized revenge murder?"

It was then that Collings began to develop the concept of the V-Chip (the V stands for "viewer," not "violence" as popularly believed). "I was trying to understand the forces that influenced the killer, and this led me into some fairly deep academic reading on the effects of television violence," he explains. He cites a study in the *Journal of Epidemiology* that compared societies in Alberta and South Africa before and after the introduction of television. The study speculated that television might lead to 10,000 murders per year in the United States because of its influence upon unstable people. Tim was shocked by this figure: "I thought I could address this trend both as a parent and as an engineer. I knew technology couldn't supply a total solution, but I thought it should contribute toward one, especially since technology helped create the problem."

By mid-1990 Tim was working on innovative technology to solve the problem, and he explored the idea with the Canadian Radio-Television and Telecommunications Commission (CRTC) when the agency requested public input and commissioned two studies on the effects of television violence.

Tim explains: "The most effective and elegant solution, I concluded, would be the development of a classification system to be used by broadcasters to warn viewers about potentially objectionable programs while being aired, coupled with a simple technological device to

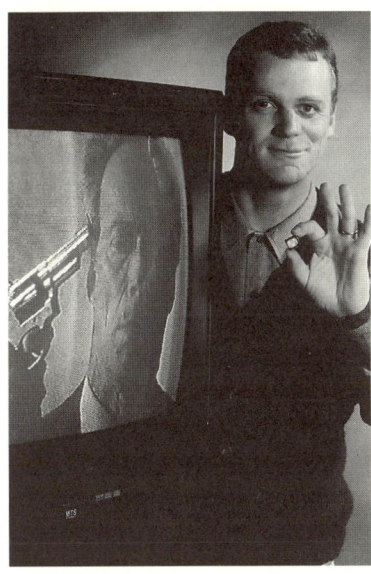

A gun, Clint Eastwood, Tim Collings and the V-Chip.

Photo by Greg Ehlers. Photo courtesy IMC/Simon Fraser University, Burnaby, B.C.

decode the system. Thus, parents would be able to control the type of programming coming into their homes. Parental warnings for programs with adult themes were already in use throughout the industry, and I envisaged a similar system that would allow parents to preselect their own thresholds of language, violence, and sexual activity on television programming and, ultimately, make home viewing a bit more manageable."

Collings decided to use infrared signals to evoke an interactive menu on the television screen that would show tolerance thresholds to be programmed by the parent. The device would flag and block programs that transgressed the levels chosen, allowing only acceptable programs through the electronic security gate. An unseen part of the television signal called the Vertical Blanking Interval (VBI) is used to transmit data for captions as well as other program information. Because television is comprised of a series of still pictures that create the sense of motion through the eye-brain function, data can be carried in the blanking interval between adjacent frames. When Tim noticed that the VBI had room for a set of program classifications, he wrote to the chair of the CRTC, at that time Keith Spicer, who encouraged Tim to develop his project.

Up to then people were solely dependent on government intervention to guard against violence in television programs. However, Tim's system allows the control to be consumer driven and enforced. "Canada has a broadcaster's code that prohibits the really raunchy programs," Tim says, "and this technology is designed to augment parents in exercising responsibility for raising their offspring. The V-Chip should not give anyone a false sense of security. Parents will still need to be watchful. I don't suggest that every program with sex or violence is not worth watching. *Schindler's List* is wonderful. You just wouldn't want to see it with your four year old."

In March 1996 the CRTC ruled that the television industry jointly develop and comply with a program-classification system for all programming in Canada, including foreign broadcasts such as U.S. shows on Canadian cable. Controversy over the V-Chip has prevailed in the United States, although President Bill Clinton has been very supportive of the new technology. The U.S. networks have bowed to White House pressure and accepted the concept of a ratings system, and Canada and the United States now require that every new television set sold in either country have built-in V-Chip technology.

Currently Collings is licensing manufacturers and has established a company to commercialize his invention, Tri-Vision Electronics in Toronto. He continues to develop new technology at Simon Fraser University, where he's a laboratory engineer and researcher for the Network of Centres of Excellence on Telelearning. One project, Virtual U, is a system of interactive engineering courses that provides study and lab work for students over the Internet. He says that "These new courses let students read other students' input and work out group solutions."

Tim Collings has been honoured with APEGBC's Meritorious Achievement Award, the B.C. Science Council Young Innovator of the Year Award Gold Medal, and the Manning Principal Award for his development of the V-Chip. Tim, his wife, and their three children live in Vancouver.

Transmitting Information by Light

Ken Hill

It's no wonder that Dr. Ken Hill was mildly amused with my inability to comprehend how fibre optics works and how this communications miracle was developed. In my mind the mere idea of using light to carry information has no precedent apart from flashing Morse code with a mirror, and that is a far cry from the role that fibre optics plays in the complex world of high technology. But by exercising his considerable patience, Hill finally managed to convey the essence of his incredible and most complex innovation to me.

On February 9, 1939, Kenneth Hill was born in Guadalajara, Mexico, the only child of English textile engineer John Thomas Hill and his Swiss-Italian wife Maria Hill Perret Valezzi. Since his father was principal engineer to Mexico's huge chain of textile mills, Cijara SA, young Ken was raised in the privileged lifestyle enjoyed exclusively by the elite upper echelon of Mexican society. Hill relishes his memories of the unusual system of lessons taught in Spanish in the morning and the same lessons taught in English in the afternoon, and the ratio of some nine girls to each boy attending the American elementary school then in Guadalajara. He lived there until he completed grade 8, and at 12 years of age he was sent out of Mexico to complete his education. Canada was the country of choice after his parents decided that its educational facilities were superior to those in England or the United States, and his father had become fond of Canada after visiting several times during World War II.

John's intense interest in chemistry inspired young Ken to pursue chemistry as a pastime even before grade 9, a pastime that developed into a lifelong passion. Soon Ken was working with his father on a regime of first-year-university-level experiments and conducting a multitude of investigations and documenting them. Ken's equipment had been extended far beyond a standard chemistry set by professional materials and chemicals acquired for him by his father. Eventually young Ken also worked at Cijara SA periodically on various jobs involving fundamental analysis and methodical measurements using chemical instruments. This hands-on experience taught him the Spanish scaling "rule of three" used in calculation and many other basic truths to build a solid foundation for his career in science and engineering.

Ken attended Upper Canada College in Toronto, where he completed high school, and during that time he travelled back and forth to visit his parents in Guadalajara. From time to time, his parents took him out of school for intermittent periods, allowing the family to travel around the world. Ken cherishes the memories of those excursions and the exceptionally valuable education that these trips gave him during his formative years, as well as the many personal contacts he developed that played a large role in his scientific career.

In the 1960s, while carrying out postgraduate work at McMaster University, Ken noticed the interest that Bell Labs had in developing new methods for carrying telephone signals. The laser had recently been invented, and light's very high frequency (greater than 100 million million cycles per second) could provide a carrier with almost unlimited capacity. Unfortunately the transmission of light through the atmosphere strongly depends upon the weather and therefore is not a reliable carrier. Hence, the challenge was to develop a means for guiding light beams in a controlled environment. Bell Labs was studying the "gas lens pipe," which could theoretically guide a beam of light for some 10 kilometres.

Meanwhile, at McMaster University Ken obtained a bachelor in engineering physics degree

Fibre Optics inventor Dr. Ken Hill in his lab.
Photo by John Brebner. Photo courtesy Communications Research Centre.

in 1963; a master of electrical engineering degree in 1965, for which his thesis was entitled "Beats Between Transverse Modes in Sapphire Clad Ruby Laser"; and a doctorate in electrical engineering in 1968, for which his dissertation was entitled "Neodymium Doped Glass Giant Pulse Laser." He then went to Ottawa to work on holography as an optical-storage medium at the Defence Research Telecommunications Establishment (DRTE), which became the Communications Research Centre (CRC) in 1969.

Also in the 1960s, Charles Kao, who was working in Standard Telecommunications Laboratory (STL) in Harlow, England, suggested that optical fibres formed from very pure glass could guide light for tens of kilometres. Jack Chambers of the CRC in Canada picked up on the significance of Kao's work while attending a Technical Cooperation Program meeting and alerted his colleagues of this development. The race was on to be the first to develop a low-loss optical fibre.

In 1970 Kapron Teck & Mauer of the firm that was then called Corning Glassworks published a scientific paper disclosing the fabrication of the first low-loss optical carrier. The fibres were thin, flexible, lightweight, and potentially low cost. This seemed like an ideal means for transmitting information, but for optical fibres to be a practical transmission medium, it would also be necessary to develop many other technologies, such as optical fibre connectors, splicing techniques, tapping techniques, and optical amplifiers.

Around 1975 Hill and his colleagues at the CRC began studying optical fibres and their application in telecommunications. An optical fibre tap, called the "fused coupler," was developed. The device was patented and given to Canadian industry for exploitation. In the subsequent years under the leadership of Hill, fused coupler technology was developed, further permitting the fabrication of a whole family of fibre devices useful in forming fibre optics networks. Today the market for fused couplers is in the tens of millions of dollars annually. Also, the CRC has made a cross-licensing agreement with Toshiba Incorporated of Japan to jointly licence their intellectual property rights.

At CRC in the late 1970s, research began on transmitting high-power laser light down fibres. Since the fibre diameter is small, the light intensity can be so large that unusual things can happen. When conducting an experiment of this type, researchers noticed that a transparent piece of fibre became opaque under illumination. Hill asked himself, "Where is the light going?" He went to the laboratory on the weekend to discover that it was being back-reflected. It seemed that the light was creating a permanent mirror within the fibre! Using his experience in holography, Hill postulated a new phenomenon called "photosensitivity" that formed a mirror in the fibre in the form of grating. The mirror in the fibre became known as "Hill grating" or "fibre grating." It was apparent that such fibre gratings could have applications in fibre optics communications. The question was how.

Initially the scientific community viewed the experiment with curiosity, and nothing much happened until about 10 years later, when researchers at United Technology Research Centre (UTRC) in Connecticut fabricated Hill gratings by illuminating the fibre from the side with ultraviolet light. Since Hill gratings could now operate at infrared wavelengths, research activity on photosensitivity increased dramatically worldwide. At CRC Hill led his research team in the development of the "phase mask" technique for manufacturing fibre gratings, and this method is now used by most manufacturers. CRC and UTRC agreed to pool and jointly market their intellectual property relating to fibre grating manufacture, which has been recognized around the world as a Canadian innovation. Canadian companies – such as Innovative Fibres, QP Semiconductors, JDS Fitel, and SDL Optics – and foreign companies – such as AT&T, Pirelli, 3M, Ciena, and Corning Glass – have purchased licences.

In 1994 CRC negotiated a cross-licensing arrangement with United Technologies Corporation (UTC) that combined both CRC and UTC patents into a robust portfolio on "methods for making fibre gratings." The CRC portion consists of 20 patents and patent applications across Canada, the United States, the United Kingdom, France, Germany, Italy, Spain, and Japan. The UTC portion consists of 30 patents and patent applications in these countries.

The principal applications for fibre gratings are in optical fibre networks. The full carrying capacity of a single optical fibre strand is enormous, greater than 20,000 gigahertz. The fibre gratings provide a means of putting several light-beam channels, having different colours (wavelengths), on a single optical fibre. The technique is called "wavelength division multiplexing" (WDM). The optical fibres already installed in the ground are being converted to WDM. Fibre gratings are also used in optical amplifiers, dispersion compensators, and laser frequency stabilization.

Photonics or optoelectronics have opened the gateway to high-speed, huge-volume, intercontinental electronic communications. Light has literally replaced cobwebs of wires and made instant communication transfer possible in high technology such as high-performance computers, the enormous Internet with its millions of Web pages, intercontinental telephone cables, defence systems, geological explorations with arrays of sensors and acoustic soundings, early warning systems for earthquakes, smart fuses on hi-tech missiles, multiplex systems, and sensors for "smart" structures, and a multitude of other uses. The list grows longer every day.

During his career Hill has seen optical communication develop from its beginnings to practical reality. A CRC forecast in the 1970s predicted that by the year 2000 satellites would be a primary carrier of information. However, in the short span of 20 years, fibre optics has become the Earth's dominant carrier of information. For the first time in history, the carrying capacity of communications lines is effectively unlimited.

In 1995 Dr. Kenneth O. Hill received the Principal Award of The Manning Foundation for "the discovery of photosensitivity in optical fibres, and the development of techniques now being used in the commercial production of wavelength filters, wavelength multiplexers and demultiplexers, laser frequency stabilizers, temperature and strain sensors and dispersion compensators." At the 1996 Optical Fiber Communications Conference in San Jose, California, he was awarded the John Tyndall Award sponsored by the Institute of Electrical and Electronic Engineers (IEEE), the Lasers and Electro-Optics Society (LEOS), and the Optical Society of America (OSA). The award citation is "for discovery of photosensitivity in optical fibres and its application to Bragg gratings used in device systems."

Hill is a professional engineer of Ontario, a fellow of the Optical Society of America, the program co-chair for the 1988 Optical Fibre Communications Conference, an associate editor for the IEEE Photonic Technology Letters and the IEEE/OSA Journal of Lightwave Technology, an author or co-author of more than 100 scientific publications in refereed journals, and the holder of more than 10 patents, which are assigned to the Canadian government. He has a daughter, Vivian Clement, an opthalmologist, and a son, John, a dentist. He lives in Kanata, Ontario.

7

Helping Turn Dreams into Reality

The Canadian Industrial Design Innovation Centre

Frank Phripp

Frank Phripp has devoted much of his life to his belief in dreamers, observing the power of their creativity and respecting their awesome potential. To this end, he created the Canadian Industrial Design Innovation Centre in Waterloo, Ontario.

Frank was born in Newmarket, Ontario, on September 3, 1917, and was raised in Toronto. In 1941 he received a bachelor of arts degree in applied science in civil and aeronautical engineering from the University of Toronto and spent the following 26 years in

Founder Frank Phripp.
Photo courtesy Industrial Design
Innovation Centre, Waterloo, Ontario.

the RCAF. During World War II, he served as a bomber pilot, and he was a test pilot in Canada and England until 1949, when he was sent for postgraduate studies to the University of Michigan. It was there that he earned a master's degree in aeronautical engineering and a master's degree in mathematics. He continued to serve in the air force on the purchasing side as technological design authority, providing engineering specifications up to his retirement in 1957.

Frank then joined the University of Waterloo's Research Institute as assistant director, and he channelled considerable energy into assisting the initial commercial development of inventions coming out of the university's research labs. "While doing this on campus," Frank explains, "I found it very interesting that the university enjoyed a fairly continual flow of inquiries from the general public, and these people were referred to me."

The first rudimentary evaluations of inventions from outside the institute were conducted early in the 1970s, though Frank believed that inventors needed a more substantial service considering the potential significance of their ideas. For this reason he embarked on a fundraising campaign at federal government offices in Ottawa and on the campus of the University of Waterloo. After a trial period beginning in 1976, this fundraising led to the official establishment of the Canadian Industrial Innovation Centre in Waterloo in 1981.

Since the centre's birth, over 11,000 inventions at all stages of development, from concept to finished product, have received the attention of specialized professionals on staff at the centre. To inventors they offer a broad range of academic expertise through their technical and business degrees and practical experience from employment in service and manufacturing industries. Many inventors whom I have been in contact with over the years, including those interviewed for this chapter, agree that the Innovation Centre has rendered reliable and worthwhile assistance to them. The centre's program is designed to provide a variety of in-house services, which enable inventors to obtain valuable assistance from people whom they can trust and at prices that are well within reason. Their services cover inven-tion evaluations, market research, engineer-

Marketing Services Group Manager Gary Svoboda.
Photo courtesy Industrial Design Innovation Centre, Waterloo, Ontario.

ing design and development, as well as training through workshops, seminars, and information tools such as books, tapes, and software. The centre also has a database of technology available for licence. The organization's seasonal newsletter, EUREKA, is distributed free to over 10,000 recipients with special interests all across Canada and is the only one of its kind. EUREKA carried a story about me in the fall 1995 issue, and the response was exceptional and far-reaching, including international manufacturers, educational institutions, rele-vant government offices, and many other inventors.

Gary Svoboda, the Innovation Centre's manager of marketing ser-vices, told me that he was originally attracted to work at the centre 13 years ago because of the wonder and excitement that clients bring to the centre's office, and things haven't changed. He believes that the atmosphere is even more dynamic now because the centre has gained momentum over the years. His background includes a degree in electrical engineering from the University of Toronto and a master of business administration degree from the University of Western Ontario. He gets personally involved with most of the projects, especially those requiring custom market research and the input of general marketing acumen.

"Our job at the Innovation Centre," Gary explains, "is to be realistic and to give Canadian inventors solid, down-to-earth advice about their ideas. Our experience has been that ninety-eight percent did not make it successfully to the market. Of course, inventors always believe in their ideas, . . . which is a strong comment on the hope and drive inventors possess. But it's also a warning flag to us that we make sure we give thoughtful, informed advice, because they need to know the honest truth. Getting this across is always tricky, because we want to be encouraging, but at the same time we want to make certain their feet are planted firmly on the ground without damaging their confidence."

The centre finds a discrepancy between the number of inventors that it assesses as promising (approximately 15 percent) and the smaller number (two percent) that actually achieve success. The Innovation Centre believes that much of this difference is in the number of innovations abandoned because the inventor does not have the financial, technical, or business support to see the project through. The centre is endeavouring to address this critical problem.

I've selected the following inventors from the files of the Innovation Centre because I believe that they probably represent a good cross-section of different innovative situations and because I am struck by the uncanny simplicity and common sense that each of these inventors demonstrates. The files of the Innovation Centre are brimming with many more exceptional examples.

A Huge New Energy Source

Alan and Gerald Vowles

The world's largest known source of clean, renewable energy, the action of waves on the ocean, has been harnessed by geologist Alan Vowles of Flin Flon, Manitoba, and his school teacher brother Gerald Vowles of Belleville, Ontario.

The brothers were born on a farm on the edge of Brownsburgh, Quebec, Gerald in 1948 and Alan one and a half years later. While they were growing up, their father was a lab technician and inventor at Canadian Industries Limited, and according to Gerald his zest for innovation rubbed off on his two sons through years of imaginative conceptualizing and ensuing discussions between them. Gerald subsequently graduated from the University of New Brunswick Teachers' College, and Alan received his degree in geological technology from Cambrian College in Sault Ste. Marie. Alan has been recognized for innovative developments in geological exploration that are currently being used in Canada and abroad.

In 1990 the two brothers considered the use of wave energy in answer to the urgent quest of governments all over the world for an efficient, nonpolluting source of power generation. The Canadian National Energy Policy mandate is to decrease dependency upon fossil fuels, the emissions of which lead to global warming. Other countries are also aggressively searching for ways to reduce or eliminate their use of fossil fuels. The brothers decided to embark upon an intensive phase of investigation to determine why the technology in this field had not been commercialized. They found that the demand for fresh water far outstrips everything else, and according to the Worldwatch Institute, the shortage of fresh water worldwide is increasing catastrophically. The huge market demands for fresh water and for an efficient energy source are poised for immediate exploitation.

Wave energy is constant and is more concentrated than either wind or solar energy, and for these reasons significant attention is being drawn to the Vowles brothers' invention from the United States, Great Britain, Japan, and Norway, as well as Canada. Fully patented in the United States, Canada, and several western European countries, the Wavemill offers these countries an opportunity to exploit wave energy easily and comparatively inexpensively. The Wavemill is a floating device that converts the energy contained in the rise and fall of ocean waves to produce electricity or hydrogen fuel. In addition, it is an exceptionally efficient floating desalination plant by virtue of being used at the site of raw material for the production of fresh water.

The brothers established the Wavemill Energy Corporation to develop and market their products, beginning with the sales of electricity to Caribbean island countries. And several have confirmed that they welcome the opportunity to save almost half their current costs for the desalination of seawater.

The National Research Council is studying the capacities of the Wavemill by putting a prototype unit 10' high × 10' long × 6' wide through its paces. The actual size of a conventional unit is 75' high × 24' long × 24' wide, only one in an array of 10 to 30 units depending upon the amount of energy required by the user.

The Innovation Centre's critical-factor assessment has been helpful, although Gerry says that their biggest assets could very well be their patience and their tenacity. However, when the Innovation Centre recognized Alan and Gerald Vowles for their development of a renewable energy source by bestowing on them the 1996 Green-Vention Award, the marketing momentum for the Wavemill began to grow substantially.

The "Wavemill," a new and huge energy source.
Photo courtesy Vowles Brothers.

Easing Pain with Hot Grain

Audrey McQuarrie

When Audrey McQuarrie was suffering from a whiplash injury that she received as a result of a car accident, she was constantly on the lookout for anything that could possibly offer some relief. Sessions with her chiropractor were a big help, but she needed something to bridge the gaps between visits. Finally, three years later in early 1994, a friend showed her a bag of grain that she had used and experienced good results from, and the friend wanted Audrey to try this remedy. Audrey heated it in the microwave to make a heat pack, and for a cold pack she put it into the freezer. But it smelled like a granary, and it was prickly on one's skin and not altogether clean looking, so although she was impressed with the idea, she wasn't about to use it on her neck.

For a while Audrey thought about the concept. Then she discussed it with her chiropractor, who didn't discourage her from using it, so she decided to give it a try. Her husband, Craege, encouraged her and offered to help whenever he could. With her only child gone to raise her own family of two sons, she welcomed an innovative challenge.

But Audrey had to make some vast improvements to make these hot or cold packs comfortable for her or anyone else to use. First she tried rice, then beans, then an assortment of other similar things, but the results were only so-so. Then she obtained some thoroughly husked and cleaned wheat from the local feed store and discovered that it had the right texture and moisture content for moist heat or dry cold. She extensively tested different types of cloth for her grain bags, settling on durable cotton corduroy. She made some demos and tried them out. Wheatheat was born.

During her research Audrey discovered that many years ago Quakers used this remedy for headaches, muscle strain, and arthritic pain. And armed forces veterans who served overseas said that they greatly appreciated the little pillows of hot or cold grain supplied by European farmers' wives for their muscle pains.

After using Wheatheat for a few days, Audrey found that her whiplash pain had subsided, and she revelled in this wonderful discovery. Having been a bookkeeper for 20 years, she knew the importance of patience and study. So she consulted with local doctors and chiropractors, approached the Innovation Centre in Waterloo with her findings, and received its approval in a critical-factor assessment of the concept and product.

On June 10, 1994, Audrey demonstrated Wheatheat for her chiropractor, who liked it so much that she immediately purchased an order, and word spread. Audrey continues to rely on the Innovation Centre for assistance and appreciates the valuable, free advice. Wheatheat is stocked in 90 health food stores, chiropractors' and doctors' offices, and drugstores across Ontario, and the distribution is now growing every day.

The little grain pillows have the pleasant aroma of freshly baked bread when used as hot packs and are great for cold packs. They're available in four sizes: minipack, neck roll, shoulder pack, and lumbar cushion. At the time of this writing, Audrey McQuarrie had just

ordered another 10 tonnes of wheat for bag manufacture at her home in Spragge, Ontario, about 100 miles east of Sault Ste. Marie.

Audrey McQuarrie and her Wheatheat cushions.
Photo courtesy Audrey McQuarrie, Spragge, Ontario.

A Landmarc in Saving Lives

Carla Hansen

Thomas J. Barnard, MD, CCFP (EM), FAAFP, medical director of the Advanced Life Support Program, Sioux Lookout General Hospital, wrote to Carla Hansen:

"I was recently involved in a resuscitation in which your Landmarc device was used by the ambulance attendants who brought in the victim of a cardiac arrest on whom basic life support was being performed. The device was extremely useful to us during the prolonged efforts at advanced life support that were intermingled with chest compressions. The individual who was responsible for the chest compressions was never unsure of their place on the chest, and between defibrillation efforts there was no problem with excess gel causing the operator's hands to slip.

I was very impressed both by the ingenuity of the device and its remarkable ability to stay placed on the chest where the first operator had put it. Congratulations on a very fine and useful medical device. I would personally recommend that every ambulance be equipped with the Landmarc device, and that it be carried by the attendants in the same fashion that everyone carries their own pocket masks, scissors, and other indispensable items of use in the prehospital arena."

Carla grew up near Lake of the Woods in Baudette, Minnesota, and later moved to Dryden, Ontario. The terrain around Dryden is rugged, and children there have to be raised with a knowledge of wilderness survival.

An attendant on air and land ambulances, Carla encountered a difficult rescue in the summer of 1984. On a call to take a farmer from the field where he had collapsed to the hospital in Dryden about 30 minutes away, Carla needed to perform CPR as his vital signs were absent. Because of the bumps, hills, and curves in the road, and the perspiration from both her patient and herself, she had difficulty keeping her hands from slipping from the landmark position, and as the vehicle bounced along the road and jostled her and her patient, she had to continually guess where she should resume. And every time her hands slipped from the landmark position while performing compression, there was a risk of further injury to the patient. It was a terrifying experience that she couldn't forget.

Carla looked into various methods of creating a simple, inexpensive instrument that would solve the problems of current ambulatory administration of CPR. She had to design a device of appropriate materials that would remain in the landmark position and not slip off due to perspiration or the application of gel and that would keep the attendant's fingers from slipping off during CPR.

With the assistance of Lakehead University's affiliate service to inventors, Carla was able to start active development of Landmarc by industrial-design work and by identifying a Winnipeg plastics fabricator. Demonstration prototypes were soon produced, and intensive testing was conducted. The Innovation Centre picked up the traces, conducted a critical-factor assessment, and advised Carla further – to the extent that the product has been in distribution by MTM Health Products and regularly sells annually some 25,000 units worldwide. For those 25,000 units each year, how many lives are saved because of Carla Hansen's personal integrity and determination?

The Ideal Housesitter

Robert Simmons

Giving your home the appearance of being occupied when you're away is an inexpensive, effective, and easy way to prevent burglaries, thanks to Robert Simmons of Etobicoke, Ontario. He invented the HomeMinder, a self-programming security timer for lights.

When Robert discovered that his parents had trouble figuring out the light security system that they had purchased, he decided to develop a simpler way to give their house a lived-in appearance, and as a product engineer in the controls industry, he had the skills to do the job and make it work.

Born in Ottawa in 1961, Robert attended Ryerson Polytechnical Institute in the 1970s and graduated with a diploma in electrical engineering technology. He plied his technical ability by selling professional audio and video equipment to various organizations, including television stations, over the years, and in 1983 he came up with his concept for the HomeMinder. Months later he finished building a prototype and began testing and demonstrating it into the 1990s, when he started the Minder Corporation.

The HomeMinder is installed in the place of an existing light switch, and because there are no timers to be set, the product is simpler and faster to use than other light security systems. Every time the lights are turned on or off

Inventor Bob Simmons and his dad Bert Simmons, the main financier of the Home Minder project.
Photo courtesy Minder Research Corporation, Etobicoke, Ontario.

in the course of one's regular lifestyle, the built-in microcomputer memorizes the activity. If the user is going to be away for an evening, weekend, or extended period, he or she activates the system by pressing and holding each of the HomeMinders in the home for two to three seconds, until the LED comes on. The microcomputer creates a 24-hour on/off programming of one to 48 actions and will repeat this pattern for as long as required. To deactivate the system, one simply presses the HomeMinder once and it goes back to manual mode and begins memorizing the new pattern. And to eliminate the repetitive look of a timer, the HomeMinder randomizes each of the on/off actions by plus or minus zero to 15 minutes. The timer can also be used for porch lights.

Simple to install, the HomeMinder requires only two wires to be connected and has a permanent battery backup with a four-day capacity to cover a power failure and immediate recharging capability. Robert suggests installing a HomeMinder in three or four locations, especially in frequently used rooms.

The Innovation Centre gave the HomeMinder a positive rating following a critical-factor assessment, and Robert continued with commercialization, patenting the HomeMinder in the United States and applying for patents in 14 other countries. The HomeMinder is currently marketed by major retail chains throughout North America, including Radio Shack, Home Hardware, Pro Hardware, and Home Depot. The HomeMinder is very successful in North America, with $1 million in sales earned here each year, in addition to the sales figures from worldwide distribution, which is increasing steadily.

Robert quickly credits his father's innovative verve for inspiring his own entrepreneurial streak. His father is the architectural designer who started Braun Electric Canada in the 1950s, as well as marketing high-quality photographic equipment in Canada, including the Hasselblad camera. Currently, Robert and his wife Denise live in Etobicoke, in the west end of Toronto.

SAVING BABIES
Wendy Murphy

When Wendy Murphy was in her teens, she loved babies. She was completely enthralled with babies. Since then her life has always been wrapped around babies.

Her father served in the Canadian Armed Forces, so Wendy grew up all over Canada, moving to a new base every two years. When he retired the family settled down in Owen Sound, Ontario, and she attended high school there.

In 1967 Wendy began work at the Hospital for Sick Children in Toronto as an X-ray technician. She worked with a team of other medical-research technicians from 1979 to 1990, when she was assigned to work exclusively with babies in the neonatal intensive care unit (ICU).

It was around 1985 that Wendy was struck by the idea of creating a stretcher system to aid in the efficient evacuation of her tiny charges. She was watching television coverage of the 1985 Mexican earthquake. "There were two rescue workers, one on either end of a large, adult-sized stretcher, with a tiny infant centred on the stretcher and covered by a small rag," she explains. "All I could think was there must be a better way to transport children, one

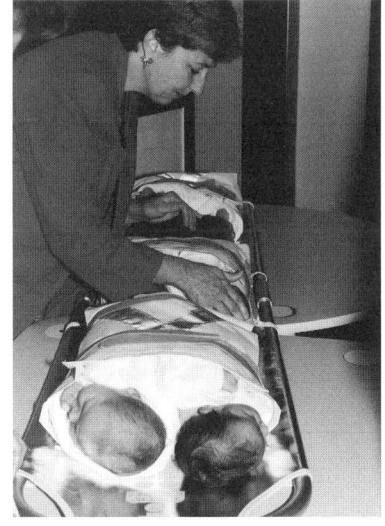

Inventor Wendy Murphy adjusts straps and checks babies before a demonstration at Etobicoke General Hospital. The stretcher is designed to evacuate six babies in an emergency.
Photos by Myrna Maxwell. Photos courtesy W. Murphy Enterprises Inc., Toronto, Ontario.

that would keep them warm and secure." Wendy pencilled a drawing of her concept and kept it in a drawer for later.

Two years later, in the middle of the night, a fire swept through the cystic fibrosis section three levels below on the fourth floor of the hospital. Heavy acrid smoke billowed into the neonatal ICU as firefighters issued their terrifying warning: "Get the babies ready! You'll have to move fast!" Immediately the nurses planned to move all the babies down the hall through firedoors to another hospital wing, but luckily the firefighters were able to douse the fire and clear the smoke quickly, so the evacuation wasn't necessary after all. At a meeting the next morning, Dr. Barry Smith, the head of pediatrics, read everyone's mind when he said, "What would we have done if we'd had to take the stairs, and what if we couldn't have been able to use the firedoors?" Wendy was ready with her concept. At the time she had no intention of seeking a business opportunity – she was quite happy where she was, and she simply wanted to give the hospital her idea and let administrators use their resources to make it work. But Barry insisted that she present her concept to the Evacuation Planning Committee. So she brought a drawing, and a borrowed stretcher frame for her demonstration, and she explained how pockets would work and how to position the babies to permit the transport of six infants on one stretcher.

The committee was fascinated. Dr. Smith then convinced Wendy that she was the person who should make the product, and he wanted to be the first buyer, ordering 10 units on the spot!

In early 1988 Wendy began to design the Weevac, and in two years she was able to deliver her first order. The Weevac 6 system is currently being used by hospitals, firefighters, and EMS rescue teams throughout Canada, the United States, New Zealand, Japan, and England. Wendy has also invented the Weevac TC, a thermal carpet designed to replace the

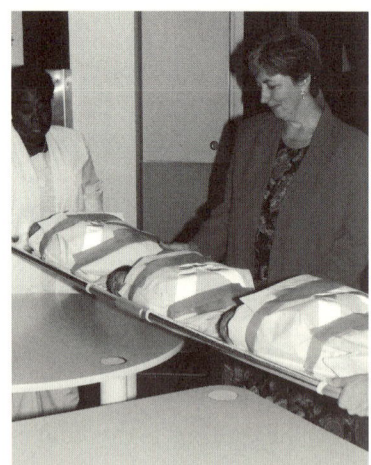

Two Etobicoke General Hospital nurses demonstrate how easy it is to lift and carry six babies to safety as inventor Wendy Murphy looks on.

common use of bedsheets, the Weevac TC Rescue Roll-Up for out-door rescues, and the Weevac 1 for the evacuation of adults.

Many Canadians have demonstrated their appreciation to Wendy, and for her innovation devoted to the welfare of babies; she has been the recipient of major awards. She has received the 1992 Manning Award for Innovation; the Sir Joseph Flavelle Award, which recognizes technical innovation, from Ortech International; and the National Research Council of Canada 75th Anniversary Award, which recognizes outstanding innovation in medical device technology.

Wendy Murphy is thankful to the Innovation Centre for its assistance and encouragement. "My advice to other would-be inventors is go to the Innovation Centre first," she says.

A Portable
Hole in One
Paul Wilson

The Puttacup simply and inexpensively transforms living rooms with forced-air heating into golf greens. The device fits into any standard 10″ × 4″ floor-vent opening and can be left in place without disrupting furnace activity while the vent conducts the normal flow of air. Level with the carpet surface, the Puttacup is ready to be used at any time for putting practice, and the device has been known to produce extraordinary putting skills for players who have used it, including its inventor, Paul Wilson.

Paul was born in Yorkshire, England, on August 9, 1966, and emigrated to Canada at 18 months old with father Brian, mother Wendy, and older brother Mark. He attended Lincoln Heights Public School in Waterloo and graduated from Bluevale Collegiate Institute in 1984. It was well before then that he had invented the remarkable Puttacup.

Paul has always loved golf. When he was in grade 9, he came up with the idea of the Puttacup to help his own putting. On that summer day, he removed a metal grill in the living room floor of his parents' home, stuffed the duct with towels, and practised putting. Then he improved the system by making a hole in a piece of cardboard cut to fit the vent opening, and by taping a coffee tin to the underside. Brian Wilson, the owner of a graphics firm and an avid golfer, realized that his son had hit upon a very promising concept, and father and son worked together on it. They made a working prototype out of moulded plastic with a hobby kit, and invited their friends to try it out. From then on Paul's Puttacup scored a hole-in-one.

That was in 1981, when Paul was all of 14 years old. While he was developing into an outstanding golfer, his family and friends took notice, and when he explained how his Puttacup had helped him so much with his putting skills, everyone was impressed.

In 1983 Paul and his father sought professional advice and approached the Innovation Centre for a third-party assessment to give them credibility with prospective distributors. The subsequent evaluation indicated that the market for this type of product was established and that the Puttacup would be simple and inexpensive to produce, encouraging the Wilsons to move forward with the project. They immediately concentrated on finalizing a prototype and developing a business plan.

The Puttacup was launched in 1984 and marketed via mail order and retail distribution through Canadian Tire, Collegiate Sports, and other major sporting goods chains. Brian plunged into marketing with ads in major golfing publications and promotions with large retailers.

Meanwhile, Paul was being subsidized by his invention to develop a pro golf career. When he was 19, he headed south, rented an apartment, purchased a car, and became what he jokingly calls a "golf bum." He entered a few professional tournaments in Florida, and because of his proven track record as an outstanding golfer and his athletic prowess for the game, he eventually became a teaching pro. Much of the credit for his pro golfing success is due to his putting skills – and he thanks his Puttacup for honing them.

Today the Wilsons have their own company, Sterling Distributors, originally established to market the Puttacup. Sterling is now marketing other innovative products in various markets in addition to the more than 100,000 Puttacup kits sold all over North America.

At an early age, Paul Wilson turned his favourite pastime into a satisfying career and worthwhile livelihood. His example shows that something useful can be invented by anyone who is willing to take the chance, invest years of work and devotion, and seek professional assistance.

Puttacup inventor Paul Wilson is now a golf pro, thanks to his innovation.
Photo courtesy Paul Wilson.

FREEWAY
FIRST-AID

Michael Joyce

It's a difficult and perhaps even dangerous situation if your car breaks down or you get into an accident and you're stopped by the road. If you're looking for help or waiting for a tow truck, what could you do? If you're prepared like a million people are, Justin Case would come to the rescue!

"Justin Case" is an alter ego that Michael Joyce created to promote the roadside traveller's kit that he invented. He currently markets more than 50 versions that include emergency items such as ponchos, fire extinguishers, towropes, flashlights, emergency "call police" signs, and booster cables, among other things essential in an emergency.

Michael was born in Toronto on October 23, 1958. He grew up there and attended St. Vincent de Paul Elementary School, Parkdale Collegiate, and York University, where he received a bachelor of arts degree in psychology and took supplementary business courses. He has always loved animals and competitive sports. Throughout school he played for the football and baseball teams, and he was eventually drafted by the Toronto Argonauts of the Canadian Football League. He made it to camp, but not beyond, although he says that he'll always relish the experience.

When Michael was a busy sales representative to Toronto-area hospitals, he wasn't even considering opening his own business. But in December 1989 he was so exasperated by trying to find a car safety kit to give to his father-in-law for Christmas that he decided to look into the situation further. He found all sorts of plastic boxes with some useful materials, but the kits generally contained useless items such as rubber mallets, battery testers, cheap tools, and tire-repair

supplies. He couldn't imagine his father-in-law sitting by the road trying to repair a tire, or testing his battery even though there was no
juice, or trying to repair his complex engine with the cheap tools provided, or plugging cheap lights into the cigarette lighter, or using a
flashlight without batteries. Obviously there was no one who really
cared or knew enough about the risks and rigours of emergency roadside situations to create and market a good auto safety kit. His father-
in-law ended up with a sweater that Christmas.

This was when Michael called upon his four years of experience
selling surgical supplies and dealing with roadside situations while he
piled up over 50,000 kilometres each year serving his territory and
beyond. And during the hours of driving between calls and waiting in
hospitals, where he was constantly faced by the misfortunes suffered
by unprepared car travellers being treated, Michael began to develop
his concept to provide peace of mind and functional roadside-emergency equipment for everyone.

Michael developed his concept for Justin Case in 1990, and
soon after he approached the Innovation Centre for an evaluation.
The centre made various recommendations and concluded that he
proceed with plans for commercialization. His first design was for a
custom corporate kit, for which he sold volume orders, and the next
year he launched four more versions offering corporate clients a
wider selection and a price range.

Michael Joyce's innovative roadside kits have saved the day for many travellers.
Photo courtesy Micris One, Scarborough, Ontario.

In January 1993 Michael devoted himself full-time to his Justin Case line and founded a company called Micris One to manufacture and market the line. With Micris One he designed his first retail product, the Justin Case Winter Survival Kit, marketed successfully through Canadian Tire stores. By 1994 Canadian Tire was stocking three Justin Case products, and two were carried by Wal-Mart, with sales approaching $1 million. Two years later seven more Justin Case editions were in Wal-Mart.

Today there are 55 versions of Justin Case roadside-emergency kits and refills priced from $1 to $275 per kit, adding up to some $4 million in sales annually. "It's a wonderful business," says Michael. "I love being able to earn a living knowing that what I do saves people from risks, uncomfortable situations, and even serious injury." Michael, his wife Andrea, and their infant son Kieran make their home in Markham, Ontario.

8

Construction
Ingenuity

Defeating Winter's Ravages

Jim Beaudoin

Imagine being released from the demons of winter that drive so many Canadians to move south permanently, or at least for the season. You wouldn't have to shovel snow from your driveway if you could simply program it and plug it in to an electrical outlet. Your car wouldn't be so prone to rust if the municipality used less salt for de-icing the roads, and realty taxes would be lower if the need for snow and ice removal was reduced. Think how much lower your car insurance premiums would be if there were fewer accident claims as a result of safer driving conditions.

Moreover, when the use of electrically conductive concrete reaches its full potential, existing and future concrete structures will be saved from decay and immensely expensive reconstruction. Without rehabilitation numerous concrete bridges, elevated roadways, and buildings around the world will soon deteriorate and become shabby monuments to failed standards for the use of concrete in construction – unless sound countertechnology comes to the rescue.

The project team led by Dr. Jim Beaudoin, with associates Dr. Ping Gu and Dr. Ping Xie, has created a formula to cost-efficiently manufacture concrete designed to conduct electricity and heat. I can't wait to see this spectacular innovation in construction materials technology in common use . . . and to be able to plug in our driveway.

Dr. J.J. Beaudoin has spent his whole life immersed in the study of concrete, a considerably demanding and complex calling when we realize that there are over 250 intricate chemical reactions that can occur when water is added and cement hardens into concrete. Because of sheer devotion and tenacity, and exceptional engineering skill, Jim and his team have created a concept with far-reaching implications and developed it to become an astounding new construction technology in dire need by every country that endures a winter like ours.

Jim was born in Windsor in 1943 and has two sisters and two brothers. He received his primary schooling there and attended the University of Windsor, where he graduated in 1965 with a bachelor of applied science degree in civil engineering, obtained his master of applied sciences degree in 1966, and received his doctorate in civil engineering in 1970. He then studied at the University of Toronto as a post doctoral fellow in the Department of Civil Engineering from 1970 to 1972.

His late father, Jean Maurice Beaudoin, was a very likeable, gregarious man who was welcome everywhere. As a boy Jim fondly remembers how, even with his strict Catholic household and upbringing, his father enjoyed a unique relationship with friends in Jewish community organizations. Jim admires how Jean Maurice always liked to build things and possessed an inherent ability to know how things worked. That's why Jean Maurice was a mechanics instructor during his World War II air force stint, teaching aircraft-engine repair and maintenance. Jim recalls how his father was able to make one or two good cars out of six or seven wrecks, a feat that took a lot of ingenuity and ability, although he never formally invented anything in particular. As property director for the City of Windsor, he was in his haven – he was also Jim's idol.

In 1972, after completing his studies in Toronto, during which he

Dr. Jim Beaudoin with a "plugged in" concrete slab, free of snow and ice all winter.
Photo by Harry Turner. Courtesy National Research Council of Canada.

also became familiar with people in the National Research Council (NRC) Construction Materials Lab in Ottawa, Jim announced to the lab head that he would soon be ready for employment, and he was taken on immediately, starting in the position of assistant research officer on April 17.

Jim's knew that the use of concrete is an economic indicator of every industrialized country, and he decided to study the "anatomy of concrete" in order to understand its chemistry, including the complex chemical processes that occur once water is added to cement. In particular he was interested in how and why concrete behaves as it does under certain conditions at the molecular level.

"If you look for it," Jim notes, "you'll notice that concrete structures everywhere are falling apart. Countries such as the United States are even forced to impose tolls on highways in order to recoup the massive repair and reconstruction costs. Countries can't afford the cost of replacing concrete structures that are falling apart every fifteen years." The answer was to make materials last longer.

The original team at NRC was comprised of Dr. Jim Beaudoin, project leader; associate Dr. Ping Xie, a former Ph.D. student of Beaudoin's and subsequently a post doctoral fellow at the University of Ottawa; and associate Dr. Ping Gu, who also started as a post doctoral fellow from the University of Ottawa. The team initially brainstormed the problem of preventing the corrosion of steel imbedded in reinforced concrete by considering potential improvements to the cathodic protection process, a construction technology in use everywhere. Because of road salt, corrosion routinely breaks chunks out of elevated roadways such as Boulevard Métropolitan in Montreal and Toronto's Gardiner Expressway. They visualized a concept that involved making concrete electrically conductive so that it could be overlaid on present concrete surfaces and, by eliminating the need to use salt for deicing, reduce the corrosion of steel reinforcing to a minimum, allowing the concrete to last far longer. And as a result of the ensuing lab work, they were able to demonstrate the viability of their primary objective by replacing the sand and gravel in normal concrete with small particles of carbonaceous (carbon) particulate material. Cheap and plentiful, coke-breeze is a waste by-product produced in the manufacture of steel and is readily available from steel mills. A major objective was to uphold the quality of the product, and comparison testing revealed that this new type of building material, conductive concrete, is as strong as the regular variety.

Several inches of conductive concrete are normally sandwiched between the original regular concrete base and a layer of regular concrete on top. The conductive concrete is wired and simply plugged in. And with modern computer technology, the system can be made "smart" by using a program activated for applications as small as a driveway, or as large as an airport runway.

Electrical de-icing has been developed and applied since the late 1950s and 1960s in the United Kingdom. The technique involved installation of electric cables in the concrete itself or between the road foundation and the pavement. When activated, heat was produced and transferred to the road surface to melt the ice and snow. It was reported to be very effective but had the serious disadvantages of high installation cost and relatively short service life. In contrast, the NRC innovation is inexpensive to manufacture and only adds one simple step for installation.

On February 16, 1994, the U.S. patent application for "conductive cement based compositions" was filed, and on September 5, 1995, it was granted to inventors Ping Xie, Ping Gu, Yan Fu, and James Beaudoin, with the NRC being assignee.

Their colleagues in the Construction Materials Lab also became excited with the potential uses for conductive concrete in winter weather, and snippets of information about this marvellous new prescription began to filter into the construction industry. At this point the NRC decided to convene a workshop with people from private industry and government agencies related to construction to introduce them to conductive concrete and to request feedback. The workshop went well, some of the news media present recognized the magnitude of the innovation, and news items began to appear about this exciting advent. The dam burst when a major article was published in the December 1996 issue of *Popular Science*, and a wave of some 300 inquiries flooded NRC within two months. The story signalled a self-propelled publicity blitz throughout North America and Europe.

People who'd been living with the discomforts and hazards of winter all their lives began to realize the incredible bounty offered by conductive concrete. For example, house basements are necessary in winter climates, and a foundation is expensive, even though most basements cannot be used as comfortable living spaces because of dampness in the concrete. By using conductive concrete, a bit of wiring, a programming unit, and some electricity, the foundation can be plugged into an electrical outlet as if it were an electrical appliance, and the walls and floor will exude a pleasant, dry warmth on demand. Concrete foundations must be built at a temperature that allows the concrete to cure. This requirement is much more easily and inexpensively met by using conductive concrete, according to expert evaluations by the industry.

Further examples of electrical de-icing, for new construction as well as renovation to avoid the premature replacement of deteriorating structures, include sidewalks, roadways, highway bridges, airport runways, pedestrian bridges and walkways, and even outdoor parking lots. A sensitive nerve in the cold countries of the world is tingling, because now that the word is out, people can hardly wait to enjoy the benefits of conductive concrete.

Dr. James Beaudoin is the author of graduate level academic books: *Concrete Science* (1981), and *Handbook of Fibre-Reinforced Concrete: Principles, Properties, Developments and Applications* (1991).

He has also published some 250 research papers in scientific journals worldwide. He currently holds six U.S. and Canadian patents. He and his wife Susan and their four sons – Christopher, John, James, and Paul – reside in Gloucester, Ontario.

ADAPTING TO A FAMILY'S FUTURE NEEDS

Avi Friedman

When the Canadian Government Housing Agency, Canada Mortgage and Housing Corporation, announced that Dr. Avi Friedman, professor at McGill University's School of Architecture, and his group of student architects had received the Award of Merit in the 1997 National FlexHousing Design Competition, my interest was immediately caught. Then I found out that Friedman had also received CMHC's National Award in 1996 and that he was well known in the housing industry for his innovative and affordable housing designs. My curiosity got the best of me, and I gave him a call. We discussed the background of the flexhousing design that he had submitted on behalf of McGill's School of Architecture, a design that he had been nurturing for many years and that had travelled with him across half the world during its development.

Friedman explained that McGill University has an established Affordable Homes Program that he had co-founded with Professor Witold Rybczynski, that an especially affordable "Grow Home" design had originated there and was being enjoyed throughout Canada, and that arrangements for export development were under way around the world. This unique and successful approach to a worldwide problem in housing design makes a very interesting story. It began at a time when much of the world was in terrible turmoil, and for some people having a comfortable home was a luxury beyond hope.

A young Jewish couple, Holocaust survivors, met in a refugee camp in the southern Italian town of Barri after the war. The young woman wasn't far from her birthplace on the Isle of Rhodes in the southern part of Greece, but it seemed as though she was a world away from home after the hell that she'd been through. Before her internment in Barri, the Allied forces had freed her only hours before certain death at Bergen-Belsen, the dreaded German death camp of World War II. As the sole survivor of his Polish family, the young man was in a group of prisoners being taken into the woods beside Mathousen Camp to be executed when suddenly he was rescued by the Allies.

In 1948, when the outcome of the War of Independence established Israel as a country and Jewish people from around the world were invited to participate in the creation of their own nation, the young couple responded. They were joined by throngs of Jewish people from all over Europe, Asia, Africa, and beyond who also desperately sought freedom and enjoyment in life. It was the largest migration of people in the history of humanity.

The next year that young couple, Dina and Haime Friedman, arrived, and their first child was born, a daughter whom they named Rachel. On July 18, 1952, their only son was born in Petach Tivka, a small town 20 kilometres east of Tel Aviv. They named their son Abraham, Avi for short.

Dr. Avi Friedman with the model of the "Grow Home,"
September 1996.
Photo by Fred R. Conrad, New York Times.

Dina and Haime were understandably very grateful for this wonderful turn of events after their horrifying World War II experiences, and they worked hard to build a happy home life for their young family. Until 1954 the Friedman family lived in a single room, about 10' × 15', built onto the side of a house. Since they had so little room inside to move around in, they spent much of the time on their porch. Their toilet was an outhouse, and running water was available from a community tap that capped an artesian well. Their kitchen was comprised of an improvised area in the room, with a kerosene-wick cooking apparatus. But even though the home was primitive by today's standards, no one dared complain, because everyone was in the same circumstances, they were free, and it was safe. Avi's father was a police officer posted away from home, so his family didn't see much of him, but they still felt secure in their close community.

As a boy, Avi spent a great deal of time outdoors playing with friends, except for the 30 or so rainy days of winter in that part of the world. The gently rolling landscape was only broken by rock and scrubbrush.

The first public building was a single-story elementary school located in the middle of a bare field nearby. The little school's cement-block construction allowed for regular additions to accommodate the steady growth in the number of school children.

Finally, Avi's father had his name drawn in the home lottery, entitling him to buy a tract home in the next government-built neighbourhood. The new home totalled 350 square feet and could only be described as austere because there was a bare minimum of comforts, but the family didn't notice that anything was missing. The two-story cement-block structure was a semidetached design that accommodated four families. There was a common lobby at the shared entrance, and their parents slept on a pullout bed in the living-room/bedroom, while Rachel and Avi shared a bedroom. It was small, but it contained an inside toilet and running water.

They constantly heard their neighbours through the walls and saw them through the windows, but this, Friedman reflects, contributed a strong communal sense to their daily life. The close quarters gave young Avi an appreciation for sharing spaces and a notion of community building and attachment that he's never forgotten or wanted to forget. As he grew into a youth, Avi spent more time outdoors with his friends, playing running games and building fortresses from the many leftover construction materials that were always to be found. He discovered that his main interest was in designing and building structures by connecting boxes with unique spaces and hidden areas. His talent for detailing accurate perspectives in his drawings continually drew the admiration of his friends and teachers.

In 1962 the Friedman family moved to the largest city in Israel, Tel Aviv. Avi found the environment – retail and light industry mixed with the residential neighbourhood – invigorating, and the experience implanted a basic architectural interest that would grow. At first he was shocked by the move from a low-key environment right into the hustle-bustle of downtown, and he had some difficulty in adjusting, but he was soon fascinated by the excitement and beauty of the entertainment, fantastic shops, and displays.

There Avi finished elementary school, which he found boring; he was a rather poor student whose constant drawing and interest in inventing simply didn't fit the curriculum. But from 1966 in Tel Aviv High, a trade school, he blossomed. He was an excellent student there because this setting gave him the opportunity to express his creativity and manual dexterity. He studied electricity and became a certified electrician on graduation in 1971.

Also in 1971 Avi was drafted into the Israeli army at 19 years of age, and in 1973 the horrors of war once again visited the Friedman family when the Yom Kippur War raged for three weeks. But Avi had grown up amid Holocaust stories and understood the resourcefulness that a person needs when in great distress, and he was able to cope. He was a soldier and medic in a tank unit, but he now hesitates to describe the terrible memories. In his final position as sergeant major in command of a field hospital, he witnessed the horrible effects of the world's first hi-tech war that used antitank and ground-to-air missiles. He was finally discharged in 1974.

Once again in a peaceful world, Avi decided to pursue his youthful desire to become a professional architect. He worked in a bank and saved for a year in order to travel to Milan in 1975, where he enrolled for architectural study at the Polytechnic di Milano. He travelled extensively in Europe and examined the many architectural masterpieces that were a great inspiration to him.

In 1977 Avi returned to Israel and studied at the Technion – Israel

Institute of Technology, where he earned a bachelor of architecture degree, graduating first in his class. His third-year project involved designing a neighbourhood in Arad, Israel, and this work enhanced his appreciation for affordability and flexibility in housing. "I had suggested that buyers should be able to purchase the quantity of space that they needed and could afford, according to their means and stage in life. The project was designed to allow buyers to add on to their units as their space needs evolved," Avi explains. "The desire to learn more about housing encouraged me to pursue a master's degree. In Canada McGill's program in housing attracted me since it provided courses and projects on housing in Western cultures and in the developing world. I studied under Witold Rybczynski, and my M.Arch. thesis submitted at the end of my studies – 'Design for Growth and Adaptability' – dealt with flexibility and explored the issues that would later become key aspects of my work."

In 1983, when Avi graduated from McGill, he married Sorel Thompson, from Winnipeg, started his doctoral studies at Concordia University's Centre for Building Studies, and later transferred to Université de Montréal, where he completed his studies in 1987 and then began his own architectural practice. "In my doctoral thesis," he says, "I developed a decision-making model that enables developers of multi-unit housing to determine the level of flexibility to be provided in a project. My studies served as the theoretical background to the development of the 'Next Home' over 1993 to 1996."

In 1988 Friedman was hired by the McGill School of Architecture to co-found a new program in affordable homes. The prototype Grow Home design for people with low incomes was sponsored by Dow Chemical of Canada and was built in 1990. The Grow Home conceptual-approach design package, including working drawings and construction-material specifications for custom application, was fully developed for distribution in 1991. Since then 6,000 homes incorporating the Grow Home design concept have been built and monitored across Quebec, and many thousands have been built across Canada in a variety of metropolitan communities. For export a prefab version has been fully developed and is in the process of being marketed in various offshore countries. A new model, the Green Grow Home, received the 1994 *Progressive Architecture* magazine research award for its environmentally responsible design features.

Over the years, Friedman has been the recipient of many awards and honours for advances in housing design, and he has been a major contributor to affordable and practical housing design for low-income families through many published articles and academic and industry presentations. He has been a frequent teacher of graduate courses, initiated special academic events, student awards, fellowships, and international information exchanges, and received graduate teaching awards. He has conducted many research projects and published related reports and is a member of many committees, boards, and juries; his consulting activities in Canada and the United States have also centred on developing innovative, affordable unit design (small size, low cost, energy efficient), as well as planning affordable and sustainable communities.

Dr. Avi Friedman and his wife Dr. Sorel Friedman (who holds a Ph.D. in literature), their daughter Paloma, and their son Ben live in the Nôtre-Dame-de-Grace neighbourhood of Montreal.

9

Food for
Thought

Turning Rapeseed into Pure Gold

Burton Craig and Keith Downey

It took a bunch of determined scientists, many of them prairie boys with university training, and lots of grit, horse sense, and vision to re-create a despised, weedy, less than useless grain into the multi-billion-dollar worldwide industry that canola has become. Two daring people risked throwing much of their lives into accomplishing this feat and have shown us all that obstacles are challenges to be overcome, and that dreams can be made credible. Dr. Burton Craig and Dr. Keith Downey especially have devoted themselves to spearheading research programs and leading teams of scientists to develop what has become known as "the best of all edible oils" for the world. In Canada canola surpassed wheat as the most valuable crop in 1994, with production climbing rapidly, and around the world canola is a major crop for edible-oil production. The boys on the prairie did it. Here's how.

In the 1940s and 1950s, rapeseed was a low-acreage industrial oil crop that most people discounted as having little value. "The only trouble with the crop was that the oil was no good, and the meal was no good!" quipped Dr. Burton Craig, one of the prairie scientists who envisaged the potential of rapeseed. Its name is derived from the Latin *rapum,* meaning "turnip," to which – along with mustard, cabbage, brussels sprout, and a number of other vegetables – rapeseed is closely related.

Now retired, Craig recalled when a simple stand of rapeseed was considered a blight by a wheat farmer in previous years. When steam engines were developed in the 18th century, engineers discovered that rapeseed oil was the sole oil able to cling to metal despite hot water and steam, which would wash off other oils. It also became the favoured lubricant for marine applications. North American supplies were then imported from eastern Europe, but in the 1930s T.M.

Stevenson introduced rapeseed from Europe for testing across Canada. The plant flourished, but there was no commercial production until 1943, when rapeseed supplies were cut off from Europe. From 1943 on rapeseed was grown extensively in Canada to produce oil for use as an industrial lubricant, and today's canola, as this oilseed has become, did not exist then. Although rapeseed was well suited to prairie growing conditions, its oil was thought to be toxic to humans, and its meal was regarded as being completely useless. In addition, because of its striking resemblance to the dreaded wild mustard plant, the mere sight of rapeseed growing in a field was enough to raise the ire of any farmer.

In China and India, the seeds of two closely related plants – rape, or *Brassica napus,* and turnip rape, or *Brassica campestris* – were crushed 3,000 to 4,000 years ago to produce oil for cooking and illuminating, and its smokeless flame was favoured over whale oil. Rapeseed had been cultivated in Europe since the 13th century, and its oil was used in lamps and in industry, in the making of soap and other products. It was not commonly consumed because, as well as being thought toxic, the oil was dark and strong tasting. Thus, rapeseed had no reputation to support its being a good candidate for the development of an edible oil-producing seed.

After the war rapeseed as a field crop gradually diminished from 20,000 to only 400 acres by 1950, and it trailed some three dozen other prairie crops. However, refinements in growing methods surged ahead, and in less than a decade yields had increased from 12 to 17 bushels per acre.

Professional agronomists considered soybeans, flax, and sunflowers as possible crops for edible-oil production, but none had the advantages of rapeseed farming. Soybeans could only be grown in southern Ontario, but other crops were serious, if not superior, contenders. Flax neither matched rapeseed's yield nor produced better edible products. The

Dr. Keith Downey: inventing canola, turning rapeseed into pure gold.

sunflower crop that had expanded even more rapidly than rape during the war years suddenly suffered an outbreak of rust in the late 1940s that almost eliminated production for several years.

The problem-ridden rapeseed had at least proven itself agriculturally, but the likelihood of bringing this unpopular oilseed into the research labs to be developed for farming crops was slim. But not to everybody. Over the ensuing years, a variety of Canadian agricultural scientists contributed to the growing mountain of research into rapeseed, while Dr. Burton Craig and Dr. Keith Downey were two major catalysts of and innovators in the canola success story.

Burton Craig was born in Vermilion, Alberta, and was raised on a mixed farm near Naicam, Saskatchewan. As a boy he performed seasonal work on the farm in addition to his daily chores. His farm life and experience were enhanced by memberships in what is now the 4-H Club, the Swine Club, and the Grain Club, and these activities helped in his professional development when he applied to the Dominion Provincial Youth Training Plan for $150 to attend the School of Agriculture at the University of Saskatchewan. Seven years later, he received a master of science degree in honours chemistry there, and by 1950 he had completed a doctorate in agricultural biochemistry/organic chemistry at University of Minnesota. He then returned to Saskatoon to work at the National Research Council's regional lab on the University of Saskatchewan campus, where he pursued agricultural innovations for 33 years.

R. Keith Downey was born in Saskatoon, on January 26, 1927. In 1950 he received a bachelor of science in agriculture degree and in 1952 a master of science degree, both from the University of Saskatchewan; he subsequently completed a doctorate at Cornell University.

In 1957 Dr. Keith Downey, an alfalfa breeder at the Lethbridge Experimental Station, transferred to Saskatoon. He inherited the breeding program started in 1943 because, as a student, he'd had experience with rapeseed. He tackled the problem of rapeseed oil's main component and culprit: erucic acid. In cooperation with Craig, Downey surveyed the available world rapeseed germ plasm and found the European variety Liho to have about half the normal level of erucic acid. Selection within Liho resulted in the isolation of the first low erucic acid rapeseed (LEAR) plants. The process of selecting LEAR varieties was very slow, and Downey created a germinating and breeding regimen for the first commercial production of a LEAR variety in 1964.

It was then that the transformation of the lowly rapeseed into canola began in earnest. Through Dr. Downey's breeding, a new LEAR variety named Span, with less than one percent of erucic acid, was introduced around 1971 and tested in the field. Unpredictable outdoor conditions played havoc with race production, and it was discovered, that the two new LEAR varieties, Span and Oro, did not perform as well as the high-erucic ones. But by 1973 two new LEAR varieties, Midas and Torch, with seed and oil yields superior to all other previous varieties, were released.

But the problems were still far from being completely resolved. Downey continued with his intensive program of breeding LEAR candidates, attempting to develop a plant capable of producing an important by-product: meal. Meal of rapeseed contained small amounts of glucosinolates, which are sulfur based and inhibit growth when fed to some types of livestock. Downey was convinced that he could find a way to eliminate these compounds in a manner similar to his handling of erucic acid. By 1977 the problem with glucosinolate was overcome, and an expanded poultry and livestock meal market was realized. The term "canola," adopted by the industry because it sounded like "Canadian oil," designated cultivars low in both erucic acid and glucosinolates and identified the fine-quality oil and meal derived from them.

The whole canola story involves the contributions over the years of many farmers, scientists, people in agricultural institutions, universities, government bodies, commercial crushers, and wheat pools. And the innovations continue. Downey has brought together a team of scientists who have developed industrial varieties high in erucic oil (50 percent) and types resistant to disease. There are also measures for controlling flea beetle and bertha army worm.

A dramatic change in the colour pattern of the Canadian prairies occurs each June when the canola crops come into flower and display their natural tribute to a truly outstanding achievement. By 1981, in fewer than 40 years after being introduced, canola was more than a billion-dollar industry. And canola has subsequently pumped billions of dollars into the Canadian economy.

Craig worked on the research tools and the technology and

equipment for the development of canola. He has received many honours and awards for his scientific work with canola and as an organizer of and spokesman for Canadian science.

Downey bred and introduced low-erucic-acid rapeseed (LEAR) in 1964, and along with many honours from an appreciative society, he was invested as an officer of the Order of Canada in 1976 – suitable recognition for contributing such a worthwhile chapter in our history. He is the breeder or co-breeder of 13 rapeseed/canola and five condiment-mustard varieties. He has authored over 200 scientific papers relating to rapeseed production and several book chapters on its improvement, and he co-edited the book *Oil Crops of the World*. He officially retired from Agriculture Canada in 1993 but continues his active career as a research scientist emeritus at the Saskatoon Research Centre and as an Adjunct Professor of Crop Science at the University of Saskatchewan. In addition, he served on the Prime Minister's National Advisory Board on Science and Technology.

Pharmaceuticals from Plants

Maurice Moloney

The story on innovation with canola is far from being closed. On top of the multi-billion-dollar success from turning the inferior rapeseed into the superior canola, genetic engineering of the plant is creating more products and a vast new potential. The ability to harness the process of photosynthesis by means of genetic engineering has given rise to the science of molecular farming, in which useful new products are made by adding totally different genetic materials to the traditional molecular recipe. It's enough to make a person stop and wonder how the future arrived so quickly.

 Dr. Maurice Moloney is so matter-of-fact and down-to-earth about his realm of expertise that it took me a while before I realized that now the bounties of nature are actually being turned to helping us offset and control its cruel, negative side – disease. "Why didn't I think of that?" is the common remark when we hear about an astounding invention that clearly makes sense. But when people hear about Moloney's innovative achievements, it's more likely to be, "I wish I could think of the mere possibility of something like that!"

In the town of Carrickmacross in County Monaghan, Ireland, on October 30, 1952, Maurice was born to Briget and John Moloney, joining his sister Irene, who was then five years old. His mother was a working mom employed in a mail-order office, while his father worked as a fitter at British Aerospace.

 Maurice picked up his nickname, Moz, from school friends who probably thought that his name was too long and formal. As a youngster Moz had an abiding interest in music and began playing guitar at the age of eight, and he always harboured a deep fascination with the sciences. Even before he attended high school, his mother was astonished to discover books in his room that were quite different from those of other boys at that age: advanced chemistry and nuclear physics.

Moz went to elementary classes at a traditional church school attached to the local parish church, in Lostock Hall, England, not far from the flourishing textile town of Preston, Lancashire, in the middle of the industrial part of England's northwest, with cotton mills puffing around the countryside. Preston is a port town just up the river Ribble from the Irish Sea, not far from Liverpool. His sister, now a demonstrator in chemistry at Strathclyde University in Glasgow, studied chemistry. Her excitement with the world of molecules rubbed off on young Moz and made a lasting impression.

From the church school, Moz attended Preston Catholic College, a high school run by the Jesuits, from 1963 to 1970. After graduation he worked for a year as a chemist for Imperial Chemical Industries, where he learned to create new molecules useful in controlling plant growth and fruit ripening. In 1971 Moz enrolled at Imperial College at London University and eventually graduated with a bachelor of science degree in chemistry. He then returned to Imperial Chemical Industries to work for another year.

At Leicester Polytechnic, now De Montfort University, Moloney received a doctorate in plant biochemistry in 1979. His dissertation describes the role of naturally appearing plant hormones in regulating the way cells divide. Moloney then returned to work at Imperial Chemical Industries in the Plant Protection Division, investigating agricultural chemicals as well as making chemicals designed to modify plant growth. At that point he developed a fascination for the way plants recognize molecules and changed the course of his destiny in chemistry to that in a new field: biological sciences. He then focused on follow-up research from 1979 to 1983 with a post doctoral fellowship at the Institute of Plant Biology, University of Switzerland, in Lausanne.

In 1983 Moloney joined Calgene Incorporated, a plant biotechnology firm in California, as head of cell biology. Here he conducted the first experiments in plant engineering, using nontraditional methods to introduce DNA (deoxyribonucleic acid) into plant cells.

Maurice then looked fondly toward Canada. Since a 1978 visit to Calgary for a conference, he knew that he could feel at home in

Canada, and because of the involvement of his work with canola, by working in the country of canola's birth he would have access to all the intelligence and other materials that he would need. At the time there were some eight million acres of canola crops in Canada, whereas there was little to be found in the United States.

When Maurice heard of an opening at the University of Calgary, and that he had been recommended by a close colleague who worked there, the move seemed natural, especially since he had been in contact with so many Canadians during his investigations of rapeseed and canola plants. His inclination toward Canada was further enhanced when he met his future wife, Erin, on a visit to his potential employer. So in 1986 Moloney emigrated to Canada and landed in the Biological Sciences Department at the University of Calgary as a plant molecular biologist.

There, a few years later, Moloney would create a pharmaceutical Garden of Eden. He explains: "As a result of advances in genetic engineering technology in the mid-1980s, two separate approaches were being used. The first was to develop agronomic traits, the general improvements to crops that affect performance. Farmers were getting better yields, and their crops had greater resistance to diseases and insects – the end products were essentially the same, but the performance of the plants improved substantially. However, a second approach, molecular farming, involves transforming plants into solar factories. This way we can make things you would never dream plants could be capable of producing."

Usually a source of cholesterol-free cooking oil, canola naturally lends itself to the introduction of genes from other sources. As canola matures it can be used to store a variety of different products such as starch, oil, and proteins. Genetic engineers identify and move a gene sequence from one organism to another. The production of pharmaceuticals is an important application of this technology. For example, the genetic material that produces insulin in humans has been inserted into bacteria, and large quantities of insulin are produced as the bacteria multiply. Moloney has made significant amounts of interleukin 1 from canola plants grown on his small experimental plot at the University of Calgary. Interleukin 1 and other members of the interleukin family are important triggers in the body's response to infection and disease.

In 1990 Moloney set out to synthesize the human gene that produces interleukin 1 in a machine that he has dubbed his "gene photocopier." This synthesized gene is spliced into an agrobacterium, a microscopic organism normally found in soil, which is then introduced into a canola cutting. The bacterial DNA transfers to canola cells, and the cutting grows, flowers, and produces tiny purple-black seeds containing the interleukin. As oilseeds the seeds also contain oleosins, natural proteins that are unusual in that when the seeds are ground up with water, the oleosins float to the top with the oil. The balance of the proteins in the seed stay in the water or end up as precipitates at the bottom of a test tube.

By splicing a piece of oleosin DNA to the human DNA introduced into the canola cuttings, Moloney directs the interleukin into the oil phase of the process. When the oil is skimmed off and examined under a microscope, it appears as tiny globules with interleukin sticking to their outsides. "A globule is a bit like a porcupine," says Moloney. "We take these oil bodies, resuspend them in water, and using an enzyme which acts like a pair of scissors actually snip off the interleukin." Like most proteins interleukin normally remains with the water phase. And when the oil is floated again, the interleukin remains, effectively purified at this stage.

Pharmaceutical companies also hope that natural anticoagulants – chemicals that keep blood from clotting – such as hirudin will prove to be more potent and less expensive than the blood-thinning agents currently on the market. The worldwide market potential for this product alone is estimated at $500 to $600 million. Moloney has inserted genes lifted from the saliva of a blood-sucking leech into a canola cutting, and out drips hirudin, harvested in the same manner as interleukin is extracted.

Moloney and the University of Calgary have established SemBioSys Genetics Incorporated and filed worldwide patents for the transformation of *brassica* (rapeseed) plant species. They have joined forces with the Swiss pharmaceutical giant, Novartis, formerly Ciba Geigy, which owns the rights to hirudin and is expert at carrying out clinical trials with the product.

With universities under the financial gun in these times, SemBioSys Genetics could prove to be a boon with substantial returns from Moloney's technological breakthrough. The company is viewed as a model for the commercial development of other scientific discoveries in university. Prospects are increasing as innovative concepts are created. Currently molecular farming produces canola and flax plants genetically engineered to express oils for shampoo, cosmetics, detergents, margarine, biodegradable plastics, high-performance lubricants, enzymes for food and chemical industries, and veterinary products for improved animal digestion and health. Moloney also envisages a wide assortment of pharmaceutical products using antibodies harvested from molecular farming, such as pregnancy-test kits and diagnosis kits for many of the diseases that use antibodies as part of the test.

Erin and Moz were married in 1988 and joined by their son Sean in that year, followed by their daughter Heather, who was born in 1992. The Moloneys live northwest of Calgary near the University, within sight of millions of gold canola plants.

ATLANTIC GIANTS
Howard Dill

> *On a small farm in Windsor, Nova Scotia, farmer Howard Dill has per-*
> *fected a strain of pumpkin seeds and named them Dill's Atlantic Giant.*
> *He has claimed the title for growing the world's heaviest pumpkins for*
> *four years, and other farmers have sown his seeds to capture world*
> *records. "There's something about pumpkins, especially when they're*
> *big, that makes people happy," says Howard, "the bigger the pumpkin,*
> *the happier it seems to make them feel. . . . what else can you grow that*
> *has the power to make people happy?"*
>
> *Dill's contribution of giant pumpkin seeds to the world may not be*
> *considered profound, but if I can consider myself an example of an*
> *appreciative public, I am happy to say I enjoy Howard Dill's marvellous*
> *individuality and imaginative achievement in creating seeds to grow the*
> *world's largest pumpkins.*
>
> *You're truly a ray of sunshine, Howard.*

A plot of land along College Road in Windsor had been worked by
many generations of Dill farmers before it was William and his wife
Gladys Dill's turn in the 1930s. At that time their main products came
from a large dairy herd in addition to a market garden and orchard
worked by William and Gladys and their three children: Maxine,
Margaret, and Howard.

Howard was born on July 22, 1934, and in those years farm life
called for hard work and never-ending chores, what with milking all
the cows by hand as well as handling all the milk by buckets and
cans for transfer to the separator and finally for pickup by the
wagon. It was a hard life by today's standards, but it was all that
farmers knew back then. While young Howard's hands were working hard, his mind was occupied by one or more other interests.
School wasn't high on his list of interests since his father believed
that the farm should come first. So Howard's innovative mind

turned to two passions: hockey, and growing giant pumpkins.

Five years later, World War II broke out, and the effects of rationing and the costs of war weighed heavily on everyone. A crushing blow was dealt to the Dill family when Gladys died of tuberculosis in 1947 one month before Howard's 13th birthday. She was only 43 years of age.

William Dill was an avid supporter of the local agricultural exhibition, North America's oldest, and Howard and his sisters helped their father with his vegetable exhibit and the showings of his Guernsey cattle. Howard was also a proud member of the local 4-H Club and would show his own calf at the fair and at other exhibitions around the province. And his father's giant pumpkins always seemed to be a big attraction everywhere. In those days, the 1940s and 1950s, big pumpkins normally weighed in at 75 to 80 pounds, and they continued in that range for years until Howard became actively involved in the farming of the giants.

Without formal education beyond his father's teachings, Howard began paying close attention to, and spending more time on, the pumpkin competitions at the Hants County Exhibition. As he notes, "Each season I would look at the different features of the pumpkin my father had been growing and notice different traits that would

help in my breeding program. After examining the characteristics of several pumpkins, I noticed likes and dislikes that I would set my sights on in my quest to develop a much larger pumpkin. These features would include factors such as wall thickness, length, height, and colour."

For Howard the pursuit of growing giant pumpkins was very enjoyable as well as creative and educational. And he was beginning to see some real progress as

Four-time world champion pumpkin grower, Howard Dill of Windsor, Nova Scotia, invented Dill's Atlantic Giant patent seed which produces pumpkins weighing over 1,000 pounds! Photo by Shirley L. Spanser, Falmouth, N.S. Courtesy Howard Dill Enterprises.

the weights of his charges increased under his special care.

Finally in 1967 Howard passed the 100-pound mark, and two years later he was growing 200-pounders! He didn't really know how he was achieving his goal: "From a horticultural and technical standpoint, I had absolutely no idea of what I was doing, but I felt that whatever I was doing, I was right." Nonetheless, he was encouraged by these indications of success, to the extent that he decided to embark upon a proper program of research, experimentation, and investigation, beginning by exploring previous records held by growers of giant pumpkins and squash.

The standing world record since 1883, set at the old Halifax Dominion Exhibition, was held by another Nova Scotian, Charles Hewitt of Lunenberg County, for a 229-pound pumpkin. Hewitt also grew the world-record squash in the same year. That squash was 292 pounds. In the United States, the largest pumpkin was a 226-pounder grown in 1884 by Joseph Dunn of Bryantsville, Kentucky. Howard also discovered that William Warnock of Goderich, Ontario, had grown a number of giant pumpkins; the largest, at 403 pounds, was exhibited at the St. Louis World's Fair in 1903.

Howard then tracked down the original seed that his father had given to him and crossed it with the Goderich Giant and the Genuine Mammoth, his father's other successful variety from the 1920s. Throughout the 1950s and 1960s, Howard carefully gleaned the family stock of seeds and hand pollinated each plant until he was able to isolate two particular strains. He concentrated on the one with the better shape of pumpkin and then determined a careful selection process for hand pollination of self- and cross-pollinating varieties of certain male staminate flowers with specific female pistillate flowers in order to produce the seed that bore the characteristics he wanted. Howard also considered the ideal temperature range and the time of day for pollination, and he found that some experiments resulted in seedless fruit.

Howard eventually developed his standard open-pollination variety, and in the early 1980s he applied for proprietary-rights protection for the seed named Dill's Atlantic Giant in honour of its birthplace in the Atlantic province of Nova Scotia. The seed performed remarkably well, and by 1984 Howard had won four consecutive world championships, holding the world record with a 493.5 pound pumpkin, and then winning a second international weigh-in at the Half Moon Bay Pumpkin Show in California. By this time Dill's Atlantic Giant seeds were being marketed in Canada, the United States, and the United Kingdom.

In 1984 the World Pumpkin Federation offered $10,000 to the U.S. grower who succeeded in breaking Dill's 1981 *Guinness Book of World Records* weight of 493.5 pounds. Then the Unwins Seed Company of Great Britain, the distributor for Dill's Atlantic Giant seeds in England, offered £10,000 ($14,000 U.S.) to the British grower entering a world-record pumpkin in Birmingham, England, plus a pair of World Airways tickets to California. And, using Dill's seed, on October 8, 1984, Norman Gallagher from Chelan, Washington, grew a 612-pound pumpkin that broke Howard's record, winning Gallagher $10,000, a Hawaiian holiday with his wife, Ruth, and a feature in the *Guinness Book of World Records*. The prize winning by Dill's Atlantic Giant seeds has gone on ever since.

Today prize-winning pumpkins are over 1,000 pounds, purses are as much as $50,000, and the coveted seeds around the world are Dill's Atlantic Giants. The U.S. Department of Agriculture has officially recognized Dill's Atlantic Giant under the Plant Variety Protection Act. More than 2,000 pounds of Dill's Atlantic Giant seeds are sold each year in North America, Europe, Australia, and Japan, in addition to the 5,000 individual orders received at the Dill farm each year. It costs $3.50 for a packet of seven seeds capable of producing 400-

pounders, and for the 500- to 700-pounders, the price is $1.00 per seed, although Howard always throws in some extras "for good luck," he says.

Howard wonders, "while 1996 will be remembered by giant-pumpkin growers for producing the first two 1,000-pound Dill's Atlantic Giants, will we exceed the 1,500-pound pumpkin by the year 2000?" He and the people of Windsor, Nova Scotia, continue to enjoy life and the unique role that the lowly pumpkin has come to play in their lives, as demonstrated by the following story in a local newspaper:

RUBBER REPTILE RUPTURED IN DILL PUMPKIN PATCH
by Glen Parker

WINDSOR – Howard Dill is famous for his giant 600-pound pumpkins. But the College Road farmer is gaining a sort of cult following for having his fake snake shot in one of his pumpkin patches.

"It was a blow-up, illustrated snake designed to scare off birds or animals that could hamper the growth of the plants," explained Howard. "You see them advertised in gardening magazines all the time." The fake snake measured about five feet long and, according to Howard, was "very real looking. In fact, it often scared me . . . you know, when you are working late in the evening in the pun'kin patch and you come across it when you're not expecting it!"

That is exactly what happened to Howard's neighbour, Sally Fergusson. "We'd been away for the day and when we got home, I noticed our pony was loose and standing in Howie's pumpkin patch," she recalled. It was late summer, and the pumpkins were starting to get pretty big. So Sally got the pony back and felt she should make sure the beast hadn't squashed her neighbour's cucerbitaceous plants.

"My God! I saw the snake," said Sally. "It was a large snake, seven or eight feet long with a diamond pattern on its back." Scared silly, Sally called her husband who arrived on the scene to declare the snake a "diamond-backed rattler."

"He saw it move," recalled Sally. "I got the kids in the house and left orders with my husband not to let the snake out of his sight. I figured if it got away into the corn field we wouldn't be able to come out of the house again," she said. Sally then proceeded to call the local Department of Lands and Forests office. "It was (Hants County) Exhibition time and I figured the snake had

escaped from a wildlife show that was part of the entertainment over there."

The Lands and Forests officer (who wishes to
remain anonymous) remembered the incident very well.
"First I drove a piece of mud at the snake," he said. "They
wanted it shot so I up and let 'er have it!" Eyewitnesses
reported the force of the shotgun blast hurled the snake
10 feet into the air. "There were bits of plastic everywhere,
and we heard this w-o-o-o-s-h sound and the thing started
darting all over the place," said Sally. "We just looked at
each other and then broke up laughing when we realized
it was a plastic snake."

"Oh I knew it wasn't real," claimed the red-faced
Lands and Forests officer. "Afterwards I said they'd be
better off not telling anyone about this thing before word
got around – you know, leave well enough alone!" Because
of the concern the fake snake caused his good neighbours, Howard Dill did not seek remuneration.

The address of Howard Dill Enterprises is RR 1, Windsor, Nova
Scotia, where Hilda, Howard's wife of 35 years, and their four children – Donny, Andrew, Maureen, and Diana – help out with the farm
and Dill's Atlantic Giant pumpkin-seed business.

10

Games
People Play

What Canadian Board Game Entertains Zillions Around the World?

Chris Haney and Scott Abbott

The Trivial Pursuit* game is so popular that it's almost spooky. I'd bet that anyone could get up a game pretty well anywhere, and in many startups with groups, I've never seen anyone, ever, turn down the chance to play. How was it possible for two laid-back, easy-going guys to hit the hot-button with a board game that is such a smash hit all around the world? Many consider their stroke of innovative genius as a spectacular example of the success that "kitchen-table" type inventors can achieve if they have persistence and are risk takers. Others believe that their success was also due to support from their circle of friends and the advice they followed.

 Co-inventors Chris Haney and Scott Abbott – with the talents of John Haney and Ed Werner, who boarded a little later on – have shown us that opportunity awaits those who search for it. And search they did, because, as Scott tells me, "Before we came up with the idea for the game of Trivial Pursuit, both Chris and I were so totally bored out of our minds with our jobs that we had even taken two night courses at McGill University just to get some relief." I'm sure that all of us Trivial Pursuit game aficionados are grateful that Scott and Chris were bored enough to become such entertaining innovators.

As legend has it, December 15, 1979, was just another slushy, grey, and boring day for Scott Abbott and Chris Haney, two close friends and fellow journalists who battled deadlines every day to get out the news as it broke and sought diversion during their precious off-hours. They were knocking back a few brews that Saturday afternoon when Chris brought out the standby that they used to fiercely pit their verbal strengths against each other: the old, faithful Scrabble game.

---

*Trivial Pursuit is a registered Trade Mark of Horn Abbot Ltd.

At the time Scott was a sports reporter for the Canadian Press wire service at the Montreal bureau, and Chris was photo editor at the Montreal *Gazette*. They had met four years earlier and from time to time covered the same news conferences and events on the sports scene, and they tippled back a few with the sodden bunch at the Montreal Press Club. Recognizing the similarity of their outlook on life after a while, they soon became fast friends.

The weather had been miserable all week in Montreal, and they were in a bit of a funk. There were pieces of the Scrabble game missing, and the contestants agreed that they needed another one. All bets were off until Chris and his understanding wife, Sarah, returned from shopping with their umpteenth replacement game. "This must be the sixth Scrabble game I've bought," Chris bickered. And not to be out-done, Scott retorted that he'd bought even more and that the cost of one was as much as a case of beer. "There must be a lot of money in board games, why can't we invent one?" Chris offered as an answer to their utter boredom with their jobs. Scott was growing accustomed to their constant quest for the key to adventure and self-determination. But this was the most fascinating idea yet. "What should it be about?" replied Scott. "How about trivia?" It was a natural. Chris and Scott had been trained to think in terms of the five w's every working day; the who, what, where, when and why of every story they covered. And from being exposed to so many news items every day, they were also expert in knowing those tidbits of information that came in handy for doing crossword puzzles and fleshing out a different twist on a story-line. So they decided that their brainchild would be an old-fashioned board game of interesting questions and answers. "It was all about the kind of things we knew from being in the news business," Chris explains. The concept was bandied around that afternoon as they sat at the kitchen table, and when Chris popped up with the name Trivia Pursuit, Sarah suggested adding the *l* because she thought it sounded better that way.

In his late twenties at the time, Scott hailed from Hudson Heights, a hamlet on the south bank of the Ottawa River west of Montreal. He grew up playing hockey and writing, setting his heart on being a sportswriter when he was only eight years old. "My destiny was sealed when I saw how that great sportswriter, Red Fisher, got into the Forum for free to cover hockey games and then actually got paid for doing it," Scott remembers. He cut his teeth as a sports reporter at the *Sherbrooke Record* for two years after graduating from high school. Eventually he received a master of science and communications degree in 1978 from the University of Tennessee in Knoxville. His thesis was entitled "An Investigation into the Attitude of Professional Athletes towards Sports Journalists." He covered sports for Canadian Press from December 3, 1973, to April 10, 1982.

Scott's uncluttered mind and dry, rapier-like wit was ideally suited to the challenge at hand. It's been said that while a good sports fan can accurately recall the year that Rocket Richard scored 50 goals, Scott can give the date, time, period, and opposing goaltender for Jean-Guy Talbot's 20th goal.

Just one year older than Scott, Chris was born in 1950 in Welland, Ontario. He has travelled extensively and is an award-winning former photographer and photo editor for the Canadian Press news bureaus in Toronto, Ottawa, and Montreal. He also served as director of photography and graphics editor at the *Gazette* in Montreal. Chris was the youngest editor in the history of Canadian Press. Nicknamed "The Horn," he is known to have a line for everything and is a newsman's newsman. He likes off-the-wall humour and tricky questions, both of which are ideal attributes to possess in designing an elegant, contemporary board game.

Four convivial partners from left to right: corporate lawyer Ed Werner and Chris' brother John, with Scott Abbott and Chris Haney who conceptualized the epic game of Trivial Pursuit in Montreal in 1979. Photo courtesy Horn Abbott Ltd.

The game of Trivial Pursuit is rumoured to have been conceived in an hour or less, after which it became an instant success. However, the time span from concept to product encompassed no fewer than five years.

Chris and Scott discovered in short order that more energy and money were needed at the top of their shopping list. They sought out John Haney, Chris's older brother. John was a professional goaltender whose hockey skills had seen him through Colgate University, across Europe, and finally with the Los Angeles Kings, though he was cut from the team. John was working backstage at the Shaw Festival at Niagara-on-the-Lake when Chris called and let him in on the exciting prospects. Then they brought in Ed Werner, John's friend and a fellow hockey player who would be the hard-nosed business end of the group. Ed was a St. Catharines lawyer with the firm of Chown, Cairns, and he had a track record of business negotiations that would set the project properly on the rails.

The historic jumping-off point came three weeks after the original concept of the Trivial Pursuit game was born. At a meeting in Toronto on Saturday, January 5, 1980, a sports writer, a news photographer, and two former hockey players put the plan in motion. Chris and Scott supplied the concept, and subsequently the group devised the company identity by using Chris's nickname, Horn, and dropping a *t* off Scott's last name to form Horn Abbot Limited. From then on they would face many elations and disappointments and be plagued by money woes for over four years as they learned that the "easy" way to fame and fortune was on a rocky road indeed. The first real financial commitment came when Chris and Scott retained an Ottawa patent lawyer to secure their proprietary rights some time later.

The next month, in their search for information without revealing their plans, the co-inventors pulled one of the most clumsy capers in the annals of industrial espionage when they pretended to interview games expert Stew Robertson, then vice president of Parker Brothers Canada, at the Toy and Decoration Show at Place Bonaventure in Montreal. Chris impressed him with the many setups he shot with his filmless camera, and Scott interviewed him intensely about the business of producing a new board game. Stew gave them a detailed scenario that helped them immensely, and ironically he focused attention during the sham interview on Parker Brothers' new product

Stop Thief. Even so their easy friendship was set and Stew later became vice president of Chieftain Products, the Canadian distributor for Trivial Pursuit. To their chagrin Chris and Scott later realized that Stew would gladly have helped at the time had they simply asked.

On May 1, 1980, Chris resigned from the Montreal *Gazette* to devote himself to developing the components of the game of Trivial Pursuit: the box, plastic moulds, design, printing, and all-important game questions and answers. By August 1980 they had a list of 250 questions and answers of the daunting total number of 6,000, so in typical style Chris, Sarah, their son, and Chris's brother, John, retreated to a beach near the caves of Nerja in southern Spain, and Scott visited them to help concoct their wonderful slate of questions and answers, which they tested on the bathers at the beach.

At that time they began to bring in sales of the $1,000 shares sold for the balance of ownership in Horn Abbot to capitalize production of the games. Their first run was financed by funds raised from 34 shareholders and from their own resources. After their fundraising blitz, they were on the verge of being totally broke. Chris saved only his cameras so that he could work again if they were wiped out.

On a July day in 1982, the boys found out how difficult the manufacturing business is. Ed Werner read the balance sheet as though it were the riot act. With the production runs and sales up to that point, they still couldn't realize a profit, and now the company desperately needed a shot in the arm.

But by then they had solid believers. Scott's father rallied to the cause, and a bank decided to back them. People who had played the game had liked it and knew that it was a winner. That was when the Trivial Pursuit game's magic began to change the course of history for the industry. Werner struck a deal with Chieftain for Canadian distribution in September 1982, and in November he outdid himself, signing a deal with Selchow & Righter, the makers of Scrabble, for the highest royalty ever paid in the business. A PR consultant then launched a compelling direct-mail promotion to 1,800 top buyers attending the New York Toy Fair as well as to Hollywood stars, and the game took off beyond anyone's wildest imagination.

Well before the Christmas rush of 1983, a million games were sold in the United States, and 2.3 million more games were sold in

Canada. Selchow & Righter couldn't keep up with the demand. During ensuing years the company mushroomed, friends and relatives came in to help run the office, more people were hired, and productivity soared. Sales of Trivial Pursuit games reached a pinnacle far above what had been expected, and shareholders as well as the owners were flabbergasted. In only five years from the initial game concept, shares in Trivial Pursuit game sales were worth thousands more than the shareholders had initially invested. The Trivial Pursuit game became one of the all-time world leaders in board game sales, and it has broken many sales records over the years.

Today assorted versions of Trivial Pursuit are sold in 32 countries. The questions and answers have been adapted to many different cultures, and new editions are continually being developed by Horn Abbot Ltd. With his background as a tax lawyer with a prominent Toronto legal firm, President Jim Ware is leading the company into an exciting new marketing era.

Meanwhile, all the partners still enjoy getting together and their diverse interests: two golf courses near Toronto, racehorses, a junior hockey team, and other exciting activities. Above all, Chris and Scott are prime examples of how people with gumption can go a long way, especially if they have the support of their families and friends.

THE BLUFF MASTER

Paul Toyne and Laura Robinson

To invent a popular board game, you may not have to be a lifelong addict of parlour games or an advertising copywriter with an overactive imagination on top of having a slapstick heart and a promotional soul, but such a background would surely help. With such a potpourri of skills and assets like these, Paul Toyne and partner Laura Robinson put their heads together and created Balderdash, now a world-famous board game that can make rollicking jokers out of all players, even those least expected to be funny.

As seasoned parlour game players, Paul and Laura knew that the world was ready for a board game that challenged people to show off their knowledge of little-known or obscure words and allowed them to escape being put on the spot if they didn't know what the real meanings were, because the rules of the game would give players the licence to bluff their way through. And early on during their research and development, Paul and Laura nurtured the element of hilarity that has become the hallmark of Balderdash game playing everywhere.

Balderdash was no simple game to create. Consider the overwhelming task of researching over two million words in order to identify the 2,500 finalists, as well as editing and paraphrasing the accompanying 2,500 definitions in the original game. Then triple the feat for the following three editions. In addition, the need for the credibility of each selection is

Inventor Paul Toyne with "Absolute Balderdash." Photo courtesy Gameworks Creations, Toronto, Ontario.

supported with every one being recognized by at least one major dictio-
nary as a legitimate word in the English language.

The newest edition, Beyond Balderdash, consists of five bluffing
categories: words, people, initials, movies, and laws. In the movie cat-
egory alone, 25,000 films were researched in order to identify the 517
that were used. The real but quirky subject matter is amusing and
bound to catch people off guard: the inventor of the amazing under-
water bicycle, the name of the indentation on the blade of a pock-
etknife, that it is illegal to bathe a rooster in a bathtub in Kalamazoo,
Michigan, what dunderfunk is, or the man who walked around the
world backward.

It is an exceedingly rare mind that can be off-the-wall creative,
highly performance oriented, and endowed with superb business acu-
men. But Paul Toyne demonstrates that he is just such a rare individ-
ual as he seeks to make life more fun for everybody on the planet.

Laura Robinson, a model, and a film and television actress who inherited her mother's venturesome literary skills, was the ideal co-con-
spirator for Paul Toyne. With his accomplishments as a Toronto
adman, Paul takes after his mother, who has an entrepreneurial flair
and is the literary one of the family, while his father is the CEO of an
insurance brokerage firm and his younger brother, David, is the president of a bank.

On a cold February day in 1984, after conspiring to invent a new
board game for the past two years, Paul and Laura finally committed
themselves to building an outline for what would become Balderdash.
At the time, they didn't have a name for their word-bluffing game, but
they had a working title – 'Double Talk.'

To begin with, the questions that they wanted their game to feature had to be radically different and a lot of fun for players. Paul and
Laura wanted players to be able to challenge each other's knowledge,
but with a deviously funny new wrinkle. With this in mind, they
developed their game to attract a general audience, regardless of the
breadth of their knowledge, and to ensure that all players would be
constantly involved in play as they bluffed their way through by writing their own answers. The more creative and inspired the answers,
the more fun all the players would have trying to guess the correct one
and thereby earn points or fool the other players into choosing their
answers and earn points that way too. This concept was missing in

any of the other board games, and they couldn't help but think that they had the rudiments of a winning combination.

But first they needed a punchy name that would hint at the fun the players would have. And where did they look for a name for their dictionary-type game? Where else, of course, but in the dictionary. And there it was – the word *balderdash,* defined by *Webster's* as "nonsensical writing or speech." But Paul and Laura hoped that it would soon be redefined to mean the next hit board game!

Within days of finalizing the outline for Balderdash, Paul called a lawyer friend for advice about proprietary protection and was introduced to a specialist in intellectual-property law, Frank Monteleone. After a short round of formalities, Frank registered Balderdash initially in the United States, Great Britain, and Canada. Now all that Paul and Laura needed were 2,500 weirdly worded and funny-sounding questions and 2,500 daffy answers for the production of a fully fledged prototype.

From March through October 1984, Paul and Laura completely devoted themselves to building upon their game concept. At the outset they disappeared into a "black hole" (they say with tongue in cheek), called the Robarts Library at the University of Toronto. On some days they'd struggle to find only 10 words, and on other days they'd find as many as 50. They called themselves "word archaeologists," became expert speed readers, and learned where the quietest corners of the library were. More importantly they became proficient in using over 200 different dictionaries to develop the basis for Balderdash. And by early May 1984, they had enough good questions and answers for what they considered a respectable game prototype, so they hired a package designer and an illustrator. In that period, the graphics industry was not yet computer driven, and everything was produced by hand. About 10 years later, Paul would create a new edition, Absolute Balderdash, on an Apple computer, whereas back in 1984 they felt lucky to have a typewriter with a correct-a-type feature.

When the first prototype for the original Balderdash was produced, Paul pretested it with his family at their cottage at Lake Muskoka, and while playing it his father laughed so hard that the tears flowed, leaving Paul very impressed with their creation.

"Beginner's luck" Paul calls it to describe when Frank Monteleone introduced him to one of his clients, Harvey Albert, president of the

Canada Games Company. After Paul and Laura fine-tuned and finalized their prototype, and made a full-blown presentation of Balderdash to Albert, it was play-tested by the company's employees and their relatives and by friends of the company owners. Two weeks went by, and then the verdict came in. Even today Paul is ecstatic as he recalls, "It was absolutely first class, all systems go . . . and we literally took off!" The target was placed for Christmas 1984, and with the assignment of a top-flight public relations consultant, Balderdash was launched the first Monday in December.

Until 1988, the Canada Games Company did not have an advertising agency, and feeling "like kids in a candy store," Paul and Laura were delighted to write and produce radio commercials for Canada Games to advertise Balderdash. One of their scripts went something like this:

> *[Voice-over in a rural drawl]: Hello, my name is Lester. People used to think I was about as much fun as a root canal. Then I got a new game called Balderdash. Now I can make people laugh at whatever I say. Watch this: A woopknacker is a slime-covered mammal found only in Lithuania [crowd titters and laughs]. See what I mean? This Balderdash game has made me the party animal I am today. Thank you.*

Riding on a tidal wave of popularity, over one million Balderdash games were sold in Canada during its first five years, from 1985 to 1990, and by 1991 the game was well on its way to becoming a classic. Since then Balderdash has been licensed in 10 countries, including Sweden, where it was named "Game of the Year," and it was the year's best-selling game in Canada as well as Sweden for two years in a row.

When Paul Toyne was a youngster, he yearned for a career in advertising. As a young man, after a few years in advertising, he realized that marketing opened many doors, and after working on campaigns for clients and seeing their successes, he wanted to invent his own product. Balderdash was that invention. Today Paul says, "My greatest thrill comes from knowing that a million people will be unwrapping a Balderdash game for a Christmas present and using their brains and minds to play with those far-out questions and answers in a framework of rules that Laura and I originally toiled over, laughed and kidded each other about, and during the final stretch sweated over the possibility of our potential to one day achieve success from our efforts. It's truly wonderful to be able to sit back and realize that this is really happening."

11

The Entertainers

ELECTRONIC MUSIC TO OUR EARS

Hugh Le Caine

Hugh Le Caine was such an amazing man. His achievements, from nuclear physics to the design of electronic musical instruments, were highly complex and profound, even by today's standards. But in his day, they must have been next to impossible for a man to single-handedly undertake, one challenge after another within a less than average length of life. There have been other people of this calibre, and this book offers studies of some of them, but to me Le Caine's story is even more special because Hugh lived several houses away from where I lived briefly in mid-1956, and several years ago I wrote a published account of that time of my life. To think that I saw and probably spoke to this exceptional neighbour from time to time is ironic given that I am writing about him so many years later and have become so impressed by him.

The great scientist, electrical engineer, instrument designer, and composer Hugh Le Caine was born in Port Arthur, now called Thunder Bay, on May 27, 1914. He was the first child of Hubert, an engineer for the city's Current River Power Plant, and Susan Le Caine. Susan taught school, although it was uncommon at that time for a married woman to work outside the home. Hugh was born two months before World War I began, and when Port Arthur's soldiers returned in the fall of 1918, they brought back a highly dangerous new flu virus that resulted in 125 deaths. Hugh also caught the bug but survived, though he was susceptible to respiratory infections for the rest of his life.

Hugh's father transformed an abandoned sailboat into an outboard motorboat that the family named *The Cradle of the Deep*. Fishing excursions on Lake Superior were great adventures for young Hugh and his sister Jeanne. Hugh created a fantasy colony of visitors from Mars, the Rishtgas, complete with a culture and a language that he taught to Jeanne so they could use the secret language. Stories about the Rishtga culture circulated in the family for years. Both Hugh and Jeanne enjoyed conversing and debating issues with their parents and having their parents' interest in their affairs when they were growing up. The children were considered exceptionally bright and focused much of their attention on family life, and their mother was spurred on to take up photography in addition to her storytelling. Before Hugh was 10 years old, he joined his mother in the pursuit of photography, exploring trick photography and multiple-exposure techniques, an activity that he continued for the rest of his life.

An active musical life was encouraged in the Le Caine household, with its piano, guitar, violin, and autoharp, and Hugh's talent was evident at an early age when his mother taught him piano; he began giving public recitals at age six. That was when Hugh discovered that he was also endowed with "absolute pitch," a considerable asset for his destiny as an instrument designer and composer.

Hugh's father was an excellent mechanic. He taught Hugh the value of his basement "junk" collection and how the various things could be taken apart in order to see how they were made and how they worked. Hugh also set up a basement workshop, and both father and son enjoyed inventing and building things together. They must

Hugh Le Caine with his electronic Sackbutt, the world's first electronic synthesizer, 1954.
Photograph from the Hugh Le Caine fonds; courtesy of the Music Division, National Library of Canada, and the National Research Council of Canada.

have made a colourful team: reserved and practical Hubert, interested in devices for specific purposes, and his imaginative son, who wanted to build beautiful-sounding musical instruments.

With this grounding Hugh's fascination with electronics blossomed during high school, and after several years he asked his family's permission to build an electrical test bench in his bedroom. He equipped it with sophisticated voltmeters, ammeters, galvanometers, resistance boxes, and wheat-stone bridges, and he used it to make accurate measurements and conduct experiments. So, when a play was put on at the high school, Hugh did the lighting and put out the call for irons and toasters to use at the theatre. By turning on toasters and irons connected to the circuit, he could dim the stage lighting and create the mood he wanted.

It was in the 1920s, during a two-week family vacation by car, that Hugh conceived plans for his own electronic musical instrument: an electronic ukulele. His idea didn't work as he had wanted it to, but it led him to investigate pitch flexibility and the possibility of continuously transposing chords while playing their guitar Hawaiian-style, with a steel bar. These concepts were recorded in his notebook of ideas. The advent of the electronic Hawaiian guitar and the pedal steel guitar 10 years later, in the 1930s, shows how, even at that young age, Hugh's innovative concepts were valid and pertinent to general musical interests. He began to develop analytical skills through trial and error as he worked alone to resolve each problem; although he had a few close friends, there was no one to share his passionate interest in electronic musical instruments.

His down-to-earth outlook was evident, as a teenager, and Hugh explains his drive to innovate: "As a matter of fact, I believe that I am and always was lazy. This means, I believe, that a person doesn't derive pleasure solely from physical or even mental exertion without a purpose or goal. I envy people who do 'like work for its own sake.' In my case it takes an extreme curiosity to drive me to either hard thought or hard physical work. My curiosity, however, is easily aroused and drives me mercilessly. Obsessive working or thinking also takes over and helps me to form concepts which make it possible for me to explain something to myself and satisfy my curiosity."

Hugh graduated from high school in 1932 as class valedictorian and then enrolled in the Applied Science Program at Queen's

University in Kingston, with the intention of specializing in electrical engineering. At the end of his first year, he studied piano for a few months at the Toronto Conservatory of Music, and by the spring of 1935 he was accepted under the tutelage of Viggo Kihl, one of the finest teachers in Canada.

Before 1935 Hugh was intrigued with pitch. Now he studied piano exhaustively, practising seven to eight hours daily, making detailed notes, and thoroughly analyzing keyboard mechanisms, comparing the inertia and the velocity of touch. This expansion of his musical horizons became more enhanced as the combination of engineering and musical disciplines bit deeper, and he formed practical ideas about musical instruments. During the next few years, Hugh closely observed performances of pianists and organists and their use of touch, voicings, organ stops, pedals, and articulation.

In the fall of 1935, Hugh returned to the Applied Science Program at Queen's and majored in physics. His work attracted the attention of his professor of atomic physics, Dr. Joseph Alexander Gray, who took an active interest in his career, supervised his graduate work, and acted as adviser for his master of science degree. Gray also encouraged Hugh's interest in electronic music.

It was at this time that Chalmers Church in Kingston purchased the first Hammond organ in Canada. Hugh was permitted to play this U.S.-made invention, and he found out that organists did not like the instrument. Queen's also got one, and he used it regularly. Then Frank Morse Robb's electronic wave organ, the first to be invented and manufactured in Canada, was demonstrated in Grant Hall at Queen's. It was complex and expensive and very difficult to manufacture and to maintain. After the production of about 20 instruments, which were considerably superior to the Hammond but much more expensive, the Robb organ was discontinued. In 1937 Hugh was working on his own organ, which was also his first successful electronic instrument. His accumulated education and knowledge were leading to the fruition of his vision.

Hugh graduated from Queen's University in 1939 with a master of science degree in physical engineering, and he received a $650 "studentship" from the National Research Council (NRC) to support lab work the following year in the Department of Physics under Professor Gray. Having demonstrated his genius by building a number of useful electric devices, the NRC brought him on board in March 1940 to work on the development of a radar system for use in World War II. The radar systems designed by the NRC during the war were highly successful and were used by the army, navy, and air force. The "268" radar system that Hugh worked on was adapted for large commercial ships and was widely used after the war.

When the war ended in 1945, Hugh worked on various peacetime uses of radar, such as the detection of moisture in the atmosphere for weather forecasting and the transmission of messages through microwave signals – similar to those used in radar (called "microwave link" technology) – that eliminate the need for transmission lines. These were successful commercial applications and placed Hugh in the position of "idea man" for the NRC from 1945 to 1948 to act as a troubleshooter for a number of innovative projects.

In the interest of efficiency, Hugh scheduled his work into a "two-cycle day." Instead of the normal cycle of eight hours for working, eight hours for personal use, and eight hours for sleeping, he reasoned that a person is most efficient for the first four hours in an eight-hour workday, so he would work for four hours, spend four hours on personal activity, and sleep for four hours. This didn't always add up to 12 hours, and after a while those at NRC never knew when he'd show up at the lab. Then he'd get back into sync and work with the others for a day, then not be seen again for several days because he'd be out of phase. But the two-cycle day worked well for him, and his productivity was very high.

Hugh built the instrument that he dubbed "the electronic sackbutt" in an oak desk about 1945, now recognized as the first electronic synthesizer, a highly versatile instrument that creates more diverse sound than the electronic organ and has a more substantial use.

In the fall of 1946, Hugh took his maiden motorbike ride, recalling later that it gave him "a feeling of absolute rapture . . . " and in 1947 bought a large Vincent motorcycle with a 1,000 cc engine. He rode it constantly.

After working on the development of an electron accelerator, later known as the microtron at the NRC lab, Hugh was assigned to Canada's first nuclear reactor at Chalk River, Ontario, where he pursued nuclear physics. From his work on the microtron, in 1948 he was awarded an NRC doctoral scholarship to study nuclear physics at

Birmingham University in England. While there he continued his extensive investigations into electronic music. He completed his dissertation on "Studies of Bunch Shape in Cyclic Accelerators" and in 1952 he was awarded his doctor of philosophy degree by Birmingham University. As expected, Hugh continued his work in nuclear physics until he was assigned to work full time designing electronic musical instruments at the NRC, where, a few months before his 40th birthday in 1954, he established his "ideal electronic-music studio" in a new lab setting. He continued to develop ingenious instruments, inventing and building the variable-speed Multi-Track Recorder and the Touch-Sensitive Keyboard, and creating electronic compositions, notably "The Dripsody," based upon the sound made by the drip of a single drop of water, "Ninety-Nine Generators," and many others.

Life was kind to Dr. Le Caine when he gave up bachelorhood in the late 1950s after he met Trudi Janowski. They were married in April 1960. He received honorary doctorates from the University of Toronto, McGill University, and Queen's University. Trudi recalls his returning home from the third one and looking piqued. "They're killing me with honorary degrees," he sighed, expressing his characteristic sense of humour.

Following a most distinguished career, Le Caine retired in December 1974, although he stayed very active, writing scientific papers, learning the Swahili language, studying music, and travelling frequently by motorcycle. On the rainy afternoon of July 4, 1976, as he drove down the highway to Montreal, his motorcycle veered and crashed into a ditch. Le Caine finally succumbed to the brain injury that he sustained and passed away at 62 years of age on July 3, 1977, leaving behind a tremendous legacy. In addition to his many innovations in physics, electrical engineering, and nuclear science, from 1937 to 1974 Hugh Le Caine designed 22 instruments, including the free-reed organ, electronic sackbutt, touch-sensitive organ, multi-track tape recorder, ring modulator, sonde, polyphone, and paramus. Four Canadian patents are registered under his name, all pertaining to the above.

CREATING COMPUTER ANIMATION

Nestor Burtnyk

Major motion pictures such as Jurassic Park, Toy Story, Jumanji, Apollo 13, Casper, The Flintstones, Interview with the Vampire, and many others over the past few decades have been produced through computer animation software, using programming concepts and techniques pioneered by Nestor Burtnyk, a quiet, retired National Research Council scientist whose introspective disposition belies a dogged penchant for tackling a tough challenge head-on.

I can't imagine how it's possible to work on the resolution of a problem when the media to work with are in a primitive stage of development as was the computer at that time, yet Nestor Burtnyk was able to do just that. And, in true Canadian style, though, he didn't think that the software he enjoyed working on so much and eventually created was an invention.

However, the Academy of Motion Picture Arts and Sciences, Scientific and Technical Awards Program, certainly didn't see it the same way, and Burtnyk received an Academy Award that he shares with his associate researcher, Marceli Wein of Kingston, who joined him after the concept was developed. With much fanfare on March 1, 1997, the Academy Award for Nestor's stunning technical achievements that paved the way for computer animation was presented in Hollywood. Such an award was likely the furthest thing from his mind when he began to explore computer graphics 28 years before, but his concept has made such a dramatic impact upon the film industry.

In 1929 near Dauphin, Manitoba, Nestor Burtnyk was born in the Ukrainian community; he had three brothers and three sisters. His mother's name was Anne, and his father Alexander was a schoolteacher. When Nestor was four years old, the Burtnyk family moved to the nearby town of Ethelbert, where they lived for nearly 50 years. His father commuted back to the country school until he became secretary-treasurer of the municipality and worked at the Ethelbert Town Hall, while the family owned and operated a general store in town.

Nestor's formal education might have ended at grade 11 had he not received a scholarship to attend the University of Manitoba in Winnipeg for his senior matriculation and beyond. Not knowing what career path to pursue, he followed his older brother Victor's example, also taking electrical engineering, and at age 21 in 1950 he obtained his bachelor of science degree. Since Nestor was still at a loss about his aspirations for the future, he continued to follow his brother and landed in the Ottawa Valley, where Victor worked across the river from Ottawa at the Gatineau Power Company. Nestor submitted applications simultaneously to Gatineau Power and the National Research Council (NRC) in Ottawa and received job offers from both; his former professor at the University of Manitoba then advised him to accept the position of junior research officer at the NRC because of its considerable reputation for research strength.

In 1967, after successes with a wide variety of research projects related primarily to the postwar defence program, Nestor delved into the investigation of computer graphics, barely more than a concept worth exploring at that time. There were only analogue-display capabilities then, so a team was assembled in Nestor's division at the NRC to develop circuitry and build a graphics-display generator. During the fray the team built Canada's first computer mouse, the second such instrument in the world. From that point on, Nestor developed a program for 3-D graphics that enabled him to construct images and manipulate them, a turning point from which computer animation was realized by generating motion through mathematical configurations, commands easily activated by a computer.

Nestor's quest for computer animation software design rules became heightened in 1969 when he attended a conference in California at which a top animator from Disney Studios described the science of cel (for celluloid) animation technique. Using the feature-length animated movie *Snow White,* he explained how all the hand drawings had been done by the chief animators producing the key stills depicting action-creative components directed by the story-board, and he outlined the huge labour-intensive element of the project in providing the thousands of linking drawings between the key stills. How great it would be, Nestor mused, if a computer were able to understand the animator's concepts, rather than the animator having to understand the computer and become an engineer instead of an artist. He visualized having the computer do all of the labour-intensive element. Animation studios would love the concept. He knew he was on to something!

His goal was not to replace the creative components but simply to minimize the repetitive work of having to draw each bit of movement by hand in the conventional animation process of the time, which depended upon registration and a variation to depict each movement. Nestor reasoned that the difficulty of hand drawing sequential portions without having even slightly jerky variances was ideally replaced by a computer generation, which is automatically accurate and would maintain smooth fluidity in the images. Apparently 5 to 10 out of the 200 animators at Disney were studio heads, and if only one with a computer was needed to complete an entire film, there would be a considerable saving of time, and the streamlined process would tremendously improve the chances of a producer financing an animated film and substantially increase the use of animation by making the technique more accessible. It was an innovation from which everybody involved in animation would win.

Nestor Burtnyk receives a 1996 Academy Award from Helen Hunt for inventing Key Frame Computer Animation Technology. Photo courtesy the Academy of Motion Picture Arts and Sciences, Beverly Hills, CA.

The computer used at first was big – "about the size of this room," Nestor said as he gestured around his office – but it had only a fraction of the power and memory of one of today's personal computers. He programmed a complete "key-frame animation" package that allowed the creation of animated sequences by providing only the key frames. This involved tracing the key drawings into the computer with a digitizing pen and then mapping the order of strokes from beginning to end of that particular sequence. Coding was provided by the order in which the animator inputted the stroke sequence, so that nothing basic was different for the animator; the only changes were in the medium used and in the control of that medium. However, the payoff was dramatic and irresistible, because this system offered immediate interaction, a dynamic asset for the animator. Instant playback capability aided the development of the film and vastly increased the end quality of the product, making life much more comfortable for the animator, who quickly discovered that the change in medium was very beneficial!

The National Film Board (NFB) in Montreal was contacted, and the French-language animation department encouraged its artists to experiment with computer animation using Nestor's software. The first film involved free-hand drawings by Parisian artist and animator Peter Foldes, on contract with the NFB, and it was titled *Metadata*. This effort inspired the production of a 10-minute featurette called *La Faim/Hunger,* which portrayed hunger disparity between rich and poor countries. After a year and a half of work by Foldes, during which he would schedule two weeks with his NRC partners and then return to Paris for two months, considerable efforts were made to assemble the film segments in the optical-printing lab so that the little film was finally completed. In 1974 it became the first computer-animated movie to be nominated for an Oscar. *La Faim/Hunger* received many accolades, including the Prix du Jury at the Cannes Film Festival as well as other international awards.

This success led Nestor to develop the "skeleton-driven" technique, which enables the animator to enrich the motion dynamics by using a control skeleton for each active image component, which at the same time reduces the number of drawn images. Today computer software has tweening packages and morphing, based upon these innovations by Burtnyk. Since those pioneering days, computer animation has grown into a major business, computer animation training is being marketed, and new Canadian companies have sprung up to handle what is now a multi-billion-dollar industry in Canada.

Nestor and Mary Burtnyk live in retirement in Kanata Lakes, Ontario. Their two daughters and two sons have families of their own. In February 1996, at the Festival of Computer Animation held at the Ontario Science Centre, Nestor Burtnyk was awarded a special trophy recognizing his contribution as the father of computer animation technology in Canada.

AFTERWORD

After conducting interviews with these phenomenal Canadian innovators or their descendants and studying my notes along with other research materials that I had gathered along the way, I was struck with awe. And when all the stories were completed, it hit me that one of the most important aspects of this book is the unique force that seems to have driven each of these innovators. In every case there was the necessity to solve a problem, and sometimes the innovator simply seemed to be in the right place at the right time, and the invention would probably have been made in any case. For example, if Thomas Ahearn hadn't invented the electric stove when he did, would we have never used electricity to cook meals? If the skaters on Long Pond hadn't preferred a rough-and-tumble game over leisure skating, would hockey have become the national pastime? If Michael Cowpland hadn't concentrated on bridging the gap between the rotary telephone and telecommunications technology, would the "tone-to-pulse converter" unit have eventually been invented by someone else?

It appears to be a trait of human nature to accept innovative turns casually, but writing this book has convinced me that innovations do not simply happen by themselves. For every situation there is a devoted, trained, intelligent, and determined individual prepared to commit a major portion of his or her own precious resources – including life, energy, and financial fortunes – to the cause.

For example, Mike Potter spent much of his life to 51 years of age studying at different demanding academic institutions, working long hours to develop his entrepreneurial skills and meeting the incessant demands of building his computer consulting practice into a multi-billion-dollar high-tech business. The chronicles of others in this book, such as Joseph-Armand Bombardier, Tom Pashby, Imant Lauks, and Avi Friedman, read much the same way, for personal commitment and perseverance appear to be prerequisites for success, even though there are no guarantees. For example, Tofy Mussivand is one of the paramount models of patience, having focused all his life upon becoming what he considers to be a meaningful individual. And Howard Dill's excursion into the uncharted world of giant pumpkin reproduction for so many years is patience beyond the grasp of many, including me.

Inventors and innovators have explained to me that they have different reasons for taking up their challenges. The personal development provided by their academic training channels their efforts, of course, and there are other goals: perhaps a desire for adventure, a personal need to be more productive, the social attraction of becoming a recognized innovative person, and of course the potential for wealth, however elusive. Chris Haney and Scott Abbott, for instance, appear to have been compelled to create the game of Trivial Pursuit by their need to satisfy all of these objectives, and they certainly achieved them all.

Drawing from my own experience as an innovator, I must admit to being captivated after the first flush of success by the romance of becoming a notable inventor and by a curiosity for the mystique and excitement that the future might hold for me. Would I become famous and wealthy? Would I travel to places around the world that I would otherwise never see in my life? Would I engage in more innovative adventures, the likes of which I had never before anticipated? Having travelled down this road somewhat, I have not been disappointed, although the major financial reward has just barely eluded me so far. But after conducting the interviews for this book, I know that I wasn't that far off base in my expectations. However, as Michel Germain of séxūal fame likes to advise, "I'm convinced that anyone can achieve anything they want to, just as long as they're prepared to work hard, have a lot of patience, and are ready to make whatever personal sacrifices are called for."

I estimate the number of scalawags, those underhanded thieves who are the scourge of inventors, to be about one percent, though many inventors would put the figure much higher. Innovators must remember that only a few can inflict overwhelming damage. Witness the world's most ingenious inventor, and a Canadian, Reginald Fessenden. He was the sole inventor of radio, but Guglielmo Marconi waltzed away with worldwide recognition, including that of Canadians, and he was even awarded the Nobel Prize for his supposed invention of radio. Experts today credit only Marconi's imagination as having been able to receive any radio signal in his "successful" experiment. So Fessenden took his inventions to the United States, where again he was targeted by more scalawags. The Radio Corporation of America/General Electric Company eventually paid a large out-of-court settlement to Fessenden, and Lee DeForest was judged by the courts also to have infringed on a Fessenden radio patent. DeForest even demonstrated television at the 1939 World's Fair in New York, calling it his own invention and stating, "The problem with TV is that people must sit glued to a screen and the average American family hasn't time for it. It is too confining and the novelty would wear off after a few minutes." Not only did he blatantly steal Fessenden's due, but he even cast disparaging remarks about what is undoubtedly the most wondrous of 20th century inventions, television, invented solely by Fessenden, who was granted a U.S. patent in 1927. It's understandable, however, how DeForest could have uttered such a fallacy – he had already been untruthful about other things. My own experience with these frauds throughout Canada and the United States has been with people who seem to be respectable, like the folks at RCA/GE must have appeared to Fessenden. But those are the ones to guard against. Inventors must have the support of people throughout society if they are to benefit from their innovative talent. If Fessenden, for example, had received his proper due, I'm certain that we'd have the benefits of more of his astounding contributions. But because he was mistreated, we'll never know what we've been missing. I can't imagine how many other inventors have been shut down completely by greedy fraud artists, or how much their inventions would contribute to our lives. Society must protect inventors against those who will even trash an innovation if they can't steal and exploit it for themselves.

On the other hand, there are many bright sides to being an inventor, and the reinforcement of family and friends when one needs it is truly a wonderful experience, and for me it has made tough times into worthwhile experiences in the final analysis.

For those who wish to pursue the field of invention further for themselves or someone else, I am providing several valuable sources of fundamental information and research.

As outlined in chapter 7, the Canadian Industrial Design Innovation Centre, Waterloo, ON, offers a wide variety of services to inventors. The Innovation Centre can be reached at 1-800-265-4559. Its e-mail address is education@innovationcentre.ca.

The National Research Council of Canada provides assistance to small and medium-sized Canadian corporations through its Industrial Research Assistance Program (IRAP) in locations across Canada. For general inquiries call 613-993-7082 or consult the Website at http://www.nrc.ca.

Provincial governments provide services through economic development, trade, or enterprise support offices in branches located in the provincial capital. The Innovation Centre will be able to provide contact information.

The Canadian Intellectual Property Office of Industry Canada has published extensive proprietary rights information in a special guide for each area: patents, trademarks, copyrights, industrial designs, and integrated circuit topographies (the newest kind of intellectual property). To obtain a copy, contact Communications Branch, Publications Centre, Industry Canada, Ottawa, ON K1A 0C9, (819) 953-1075, or consult the Website at http://xinfo.ic.gc.ca/ic-data/marketplace/cipo/

As co-inventors my wife, Lise, and I are well along the way in the development of an innovative product. It looks like this project could make a lot of money and be a great adventure for us both if we can achieve what we hope to. That certainly does have a familiar ring to it! But if everything works out, I'll be sure to keep you posted.

In the meantime . . . happy trail-blazing.

Appendix I

Chronology of 100 Notable Canadian Innovations

1796	Mcintosh apple	John McIntosh
1833	First Atlantic steamship	Samuel Cunard
1833	Screw propeller	John Patch
1835	Washing machine	James Brown
1838	Newsprint	Charles Fenerty
1842	Compound steam engine	Benjamin Franklin Tibbett
1843	Rust-resistent red Fife wheat	David Fife
1846	Kerosene	Dr. Abraham Gesner
1852	Undersea telegraph cable	Frederick Newton Gisborne
1856	First commercial oil well	James Miller Williams
1857	Railway sleeper car	Samuel Sharp
1858	Air-conditioned railway coach	Henry Ruttan
1859	Foghorn	Robert Foulis
1868	Locomotive braking system	W.A. Robinson

In 1868 John Forbes invented the spring ice skate, which was firmly attached to the boot without straps and buckles. Manufactured by Starr Skates of Dartmouth, NS, it was the world's first, becoming so popular that with it came covered rinks and the development of hockey.

1869	Half-tone engraving	Georges Edouard Desbarats
1869	Rotary snowplow for railroads	J.E. Elliott
1876	Telephone	Alexander Graham Bell
1878	Telephone handset	Cyril Duquet
1878	Standard time	Sir Sandford Fleming

| 1883 | Electric streetcar | John Joseph Wright |
| 1885 | Cosmetic to improve complexion | Isabella Cornell |

In 1888 J.A. Whelpey invented skates to be clamped onto winter footwear, as well as elongated blade skates, the forerunners of today's speed skates.

1889	Phonograph	Alexander Graham Bell & Emile Berliner
1892	Carbide and acetylene	Thomas L. Willson
1900	Wireless radio	Reginald A. Fessenden
1903	Commercial motion picture	Clifford Sifton
1905	Five-pin bowling	Tommy Ryan
1908	Robertson screwdriver	Peter L. Robertson
1908	Marquis wheat	Sir Charles Saunders
1913	Railway-car brake	George B. Dorey
1915	Macpherson gas mask	Dr. Cluny Macpherson

In 1921 Dr. Frederick Banting, a Canadian medical doctor, was the co-inventor of insulin. Along with Drs. Best and Collip, he developed a method of extracting insulin from the human pancreas and purifying it so that it could be injected into the blood of patients to control their diabetes.

1922	Snowmobile	Joseph-Armand Bombardier
1922	Variable-pitch propeller	Walter Rupert Turnbull
1924	Wirephoto	Sir Williamson Stephenson
1925	Amplifying radio tube for AC power	Edward Samuel Rogers
1925	Snowblower	Arthur Sicard

Norman Bethune served the wounded in three wars and was known on three continents. He became a surgeon, like his grandfather, who was the first Dr. Norman Bethune. During the late 1920s, the younger Bethune invented more than a dozen medical instruments.

1925	Zipper	Gideon Sundback
1927	Television	Reginald A. Fessenden
1929	Frozen food	Dr. Archibald Huntsman

1930	Pablum	Drs. Alan Brown, Frederick Tisdall, & Theodore Drake
1932	Table-top hockey game	Don Munro
1935	Artificial vanilla	George Tomlinson II
1936	"Norseman" bush aircraft	Robert Noorduyn

Dr. James Hillier of Brantford, ON, invented the electron microscope in 1937. It enabled magnification of up to two million times. The device shoots electrons at the specimen instead of manipulating light rays to obtain an image.

1938	Self-propelled combine	Thomas Carroll
1939	Process for making magnesium	Dr. Lloyd M. Pidgeon
1940	Paint roller	Norman Breakey
1941	Franks antigravity flying suit	Wilbur R. Franks
1942	Walkie-talkie	Donald L. Hings
1945	Electrothermal aircraft de-icing	T.R. Griffith & J.L. Orr
1945	Electronic music	Hugh Le Caine
1947	Electronic flight simulator	CAE Electronics Limited
1947	Radar profile (mapping) recorder	National Research Council of Canada
1949-52	Hydrometallurgy of nickel & copper	Dr. F.A.S. Forward
1949	Jetliner	James Floyd
1950	Polyethylene garbage bag	Harry Wazylyk
1950	Disposable-bag nurser	Jean Saint-Germain

In 1951, under the guidance of Dr. Harold Johns, Canadian scientists and doctors developed cobalt 60 beam radiation therapy to treat patients for cancer. Cobalt is 300 times more powerful than radium, is safer, and is 1/6,000th of the cost.

1957	Tuck-away-handle beer carton	Steve Pasjac

In 1957 northern Canadian trapper Frank Conibear invented the trap that kills fur-bearing animals instantly, the world's first humane animal trap.

1957	Automatic postal sorter	Maurice Levy

In 1957 Uno Vilho Helava, a National Research Council of Canada scientist, designed a computerized system to produce maps from aerial photographs. Prior to this he invented the analytical plotter, a device that increases the accuracy and speed of mapmaking and improves measurements taken from aerial and satellite photographs.

1959	Muskol insect repellent	Charles Coll
1959	Jolly jumper	Olivia Poole

In the early 1960s, Barbara Bain invented the mixed-leukocyte culture that enables doctors to perform a procedure to accurately determine the suitability of a bone marrow donor for transplant and thereby minimize the possibility of tissue rejection.

1960	IMAX projector	William Shaw

Montreal Canadiens goalie Jacques Plante invented the goalie mask in 1960. He collaborated with Fibreglass Canada to produce the first goalie mask and wore it during play of the 1960 Stanley Cup playoffs.

1962	CANDU Reactor	Atomic Energy of Canada Ltd.
1963	Perforated breakwater	G.E. Jarlan
1965	Crash-position indicator	H.T. Stevinson

In the 1960s Dr. Terry Allen, a teacher and researcher in the University of Alberta Pharmacology Department, pioneered developments in the use of liposomes, microscopic lipid spheres like tiny soap bubbles, to be used as a drug-delivery system in the treatment of cancer and other diseases. She developed a new type of liposome by modifying the structure of the outer membrane so that the body no longer treats liposomes as foreign invaders.

1965-66	Rapeseed testing process	Dr. Keith Downey
1967	Agrifoam crop cold protector	D. Siminovitch & J.W. Butler
1967	Pictographs for public signs	Paul Arthur

In 1968, when Richard Keefer invented the Keefer battery, he was 17 years of age. The Keefer battery is a fuel cell that runs on carbohydrates found in almost anything from leaves to garbage; it runs much longer than conventional batteries and costs about the same.

1970	Maple-sap tapping method	Denis Desilets
1970	SLICKLICKER (oil-spill cleanup)	Richard Sewell

In 1970 Olympic sailors Bruce Kirby, Hans Fogh, and Ian Bruce co-invented the Laser sailboat, a sleek, international-class, car-top sailboat that holds two people. Low maintenance by design, it costs less than others of comparable size.

1971	Biodegradable plastics	Dr. James Guillet

In 1971 Helmut Lucas developed the first electrically powered, child-sized prosthetic hand. His design became the first commercially produced prosthetic child's hand anywhere and has been extensively exported around the world.

1972	Geostationary comm. satellite	Telesat Canada
1972	Polypump liquid dispenser	Harold Humphrey
1972	Computerized braille	Roland Galarneau
1973	Roadway guardrail	Lloyd Pinkney, Gordon Basso, & Fred McCaffrey
1974	Stol Airtransit	De Havilland Aircraft
1974	Tone-to-pulse telecom converter	Michael Cowpland
1975	Treatment for sick elm trees	Kondo, Jorgensen, and Roy
1975	CANADARM robotic tool	Spar Aerospace/NRC

In 1982 Dr. Phil Gold pioneered the highly complex and imaginative development of the first blood test for certain types of cancer. He received the Principal Manning Award.

1982	Emulsified rubber asphalt	Elaine Thompson
1983	Film colourization	Wilson Markle

In 1984 Dennis Colonello, a chiropractor in the northern Ontario town of Englehart, invented the hugely successful moulded plastic device used for home exercising called the abdomenizer.

1986	Able Walker	Norm Rolston

In 1986 Don Arney of Richmond, B.C., saw the need for improved fire-fighting equipment and designed, developed, and marketed what has become the world standard for helicopter fire-fighting buckets. He received the Manning Award of Merit.

| 1990 | Wayne Gretzky's Overtime Hockey | Harold Albrecht |
| 1992 | Advanced space-vision system | NRC/Canadian Space Agency |

In 1992 Janice and Patricia Cuthbert invented the phytotron module, the environmentally controlled agricultural research laboratory for use in space.

APPENDIX 2
High-Technology Innovation

The era of high technology intensifies every year as each innovation inspires new directions in which to develop, and new growth is generated. In order to accurately portray Canada's participation, I invited Denzil Doyle, one of the country's leading high-technology authorities and an innovative leader himself, to contribute to this section.

Denzil J. Doyle received a bachelor of science degree (honours) in electrical engineering at Queen's University in 1956 and began his career as a design engineer with Computing Devices of Canada Limited (1956-57) and with the Defence Research Board (1957-63). In 1963 he established a sales office for Digital Equipment Corporation in Ottawa, which had evolved by 1981 into a multifaceted corporation with sales in excess of $160 million and employment in excess of 1,600 people. In 1982 Denzil formed Doyletech Corporation, which specializes in the planning of new business ventures and in the creation of management tools for technology-intensive firms. He has served as an adviser to all three levels of government, and he assisted Saskatchewan in implementing a comprehensive technology strategy that resulted in the creation of more than 50 firms over a four-year period. He holds directorships with several technology corporations and has served on the National Research Council of Canada. He is co-founder and chairman of Instantel Incorporated, a manufacturer of portable seismographs and tracking systems. In recognition of his pioneering of the Ottawa-Carleton high-technology community, he received an honorary doctorate of engineering from Carleton University in 1981. In 1994 he co-founded Capital Alliance Ventures Incorporated, an Ottawa-based venture capital company specializing in high-technology investments, and he is chairman of the firm. Denzil offers the following description of Canada's role in the high-technology industry.

The Significance of Canada's Contribution to
High-Technology on a Global Basis

Canada's major contribution to the world of high-technology has been in the field of telecommunications. It began in the early 1970s when the computer and telephone industries became more dependent on each other.

Computer manufacturers realized that their machines had to be accessible from remote locations, so they built in interfaces that allowed them to communicate with each other (and with other digital devices) over conventional telephone lines. At the time telephone-equipment manufacturers realized that they must utilize the power of computers to accomplish the switching and distribution of the increased telephone traffic, particularly the data traffic, which was a new requirement for them.

Canada was in an excellent position to capitalize on this convergence of technologies. Although it did not have a significant home-grown computer-manufacturing capability, it had a world-class telephone-equipment manufacturing capability in Northern Electric (now Nortel). It also had some unique domestic requirements that provided an excellent test bed for exploiting the two technologies.

Those unique requirements were related mainly to Canada's vast geography and low population density. Canadian institutions such as the banks and the airlines insisted on being able to communicate from one end of the country to the other just as reliably and just as inexpensively as their U.S. counterparts could. Northern realized early in the game that it would have to use its existing network of land lines and microwave links more efficiently. The company pioneered a technology known as "packet switching," which allowed messages to be bundled into packets that could be routed over the appropriate facilities at very high speed in a time-multiplexed fashion. This required the development of packet switching protocols (X-25 was one of the earliest) and the widespread digitization of the information to be transmitted.

The name Northern became synonymous with digital communications. In the early 1970s, the company expanded beyond the Canadian market and established worldwide research, manufacturing, and distribution facilities. Its main research lab, which had been established in Ottawa in 1962, was also expanded into Bell-Northern Research (now Nortel Technologies) in 1969. A semiconductor-manufacturing facility (Microsystems International Ltd.) was established in Ottawa in the early 1970s, but it was closed down in 1974 because of fierce competition in that industry and because Northern decided to focus its attention on systems as opposed to components. That closure had a dramatic effect on Ottawa's (and Canada's) technology industry, because many key MIL employees went on to form companies such as Mitel Corporation, and they in turn spawned other companies such as Corel Corporation and Newbridge Networks Corporation.

Canadian exports of telecommunications hardware and software are currently in the range of $10 billion per year. In addition to Nortel and Newbridge, there are several niche players such as SR Telecom and Plaintree Systems.

Much of the credit for Canada's contribution to the worldwide pool of telecommunications expertise must lie with the Northern managers who foresaw the opportunity presented to them by the convergence of the computer and telephone industries. It is also an example of where Canada's unusual geography actually worked in its favour.

APPENDIX 3
The Canadian Advanced Technology Association 1997 Innovation Awards

Canadian innovators have made exceptional contributions to existing and emerging developments in high-technology around the world. The Canadian Advanced Technology Association receives nominations for innovation awards each year from members of the industry, and in 1997 eight Canadian firms were honoured for their advances.

INVESTIGAIDE SOFTWARE, OTTAWA, ON, for its production of a new software program that couples artificial intelligence with detectives' experience to help identify criminals. Under most conditions the software makes recommendations on the characteristics of the perpetrator and helps in compiling a list of potential suspects.

SPECTRUM SIGNAL PROCESSING, BURNABY, BC. Nortel introduced a computer-telephony-integration product, "Communicator," developed by Spectrum, that defines a new market segment bridging the gap between PBXs and the enterprise desktop. By using the same digital telephone lines that the Nortel handset already runs to the desktop, Communicator users have access to high-speed videoconferencing, fax and data capabilities, and Windows control of voicemail without the cost or inconvenience of installing additional analogue phone lines.

SHANA CORPORATION, EDMONTON, AB, for its electronic-forms technology that produced "Informed," the only electronic-forms package that can offer true cross-platform functionality between Windows and Mac OS computers. Shana Corporation now has a customer base of 80,000 users in 64 countries and was recently chosen by NASA as its agency-wide standard for electronic forms.

ALEX INFORMATICS INC., LACHINE, QC, has combined parallel-computing technology with powerful multimedia file servers to build powerful and popular systems for digital information retrieval. Unlike other computer systems that rely on one central processor, the Alex system is based on computers that use many processors, each with its own memory, that work in parallel to share the load.

AUTHENTEX SOFTWARE CORPORATION, KANATA, ON. Authentex-DataSAFE allows users to easily store, receive, or transmit information over the Internet or corporate intranets and to secure it on a PC or LAN server. Authentex's ThunderByte Anti-Virus for MS Exchange client software annihilates e-mail file attachments containing viruses before the documents are opened and immediately notifies the e-mail originator and recipient(s) if a virus is identified or suspected.

COMPUTER TALK TECHNOLOGY INC., RICHMOND HILL, ON, developed and introduced ICE (Intelligent Call Exchange), a small PC-based call-centre system, in 1992, a breakthrough in the technology of automated call distribution in view of its completely open architecture and use of industry-standard PC components. The system is in use by the Bank of Montreal and TD Bank.

DELTA ENGINEERING, OTTAWA, ON, developed a wastewater treatment process (Snowfluent) that is economical and more effective than tertiary-level treatment plants. The process is applicable, in addition to community wastewater, to various wastewater streams, such as those from mining, agriculture, leachate ponds, and industrial sources. It involves the winter treatment of wastewater by freezing and snow making.

FORENSIC TECHNOLOGY (WAI) INC., MONTREAL, QC. Forensic Technology developed the Integrated Ballistics Identification System for capturing, storing, and analyzing the images of bullets and cartridge cases and linking these images to suspect firearms for the solution of crimes. Known as IBIS, it is the only fully automated system capable of analyzing the images of cartridge cases, bullet fragments, damaged bullets, and pristine bullets.

Appendix 4
Canadian Nobel Laureates

Alfred B. Nobel (1833-96), the inventor of dynamite, bequeathed $9 million, the interest of which was to be distributed yearly to those who most benefited humanity in physics, chemistry, medicine-physiology, literature, and the promotion of peace.

1908	Sir Ernest Rutherford	Chemistry
1923	Dr. Frederick J. Banting Dr. J.J.R. Macleod Dr. James B. Collip	Medicine *For the discovery and physiology of insulin*
1949	William Giaugue	Chemistry
1957	Lester B. Pearson	Peace
1971	Dr. Gerhard Herzberg	Chemistry *For his contributions to the knowledge of electronic structure and geometry of molecules, particularly free radicals*
1976	Saul Bellow	Literature
1981	Dr. David Hubel	Medicine
1981	Arthur Schawlow	Physics
1983	Henry Taube	Chemistry
1986	Dr. John Polanyi	Chemistry *For contributions concerning the dynamics of elementary chemical reactions*
1989	Sydney Altman	Chemistry
1990	Richard Taylor	Physics
1992	Rudolph Marcus	Chemistry
1993	Dr. Michael Smith	Chemistry *Co-winner for work on genetic codes*
1994	Bertram Brockhouse	Physics *Co-winner for study on atoms*

Appendix 5

The Canadian Science and Engineering Hall of Fame

The National Research Council of Canada announced the establishment of the Canadian Science and Engineering Hall of Fame on April 6, 1992, for the purpose of honouring Canadians who have "contributed to Canada's rich heritage in scientific, engineering and technological achievement, and encourage young Canadians to pursue careers in science, engineering and technology." The Hall of Fame is now under the custodianship of the National Museum of Science and Technology in Ottawa. The 20 inductees are listed below.

Maude Abbott (1869-1940)	*Pathologist and specialist in congenital heart disease*
Sir Frederick Banting (1891-1941)	*Co-discoverer of insulin and Nobel laureate*
Alexander Graham Bell (1847-1922)	*Inventor of the telephone*
Joseph-Armand Bombardier (1907-64)	*Inventor of the snowmobile*
Reginald A. Fessenden (1866-1932)	*Pioneer in the development of radio*
Sir Sandford Fleming (1827-1915)	*Architect of the transcontinental railway and inventor of standard time*
Gerald Heffernan (1919-)	*For innovation in steel production, developer of the environmentally friendly "minimill" for recycling*
Gerhard Herzberg (1904-)	*Astrophysicist and Nobel laureate*
Sir William Logan (1798-1875)	*First director of the Geological Survey of Canada*

Elizabeth "Elsie" MacGill	*Aeronautical engineer, oversaw WWII production of Hawker Hurricane fighter aircraft*
Frère Marie-Victorin (1885-1944)	*Botanist, author, and teacher*
Andrew G.L. MacNaughton (1887-1966)	*Inventor of cathode ray-detection finder, and a military leader*
Margaret Newton (1887-1971)	*Plant pathologist who developed techniques to combat wheat rust*
Joseph-Alphonse Ouimet	*Inventor, engineer, and CBC president*
Wilder Penfield (1891-1976)	*Neurosurgeon who developed surgical treatments for epilepsy*
John Polanyi (1929-)	*Nobel laureate whose work contributed to the development of laser chemistry*
Edgar William Richard Steacie (1900-62)	*Researcher (free radical chemistry), educator, and former president of the National Research Council*
Wallace Turnbull (1870-1954)	*Inventor of the variable-pitch propeller*
George J. Klein (1904-92)	*Design engineer, the most productive inventor in 20th-century Canada*
Hugh Le Caine (1914-77)	*Inventor of electronic music synthesizer, touch-sensitive keyboard, and variable speed multitrack tape recorder*

Appendix 6

The Canada Council for the Arts 1997 Killam Prize Winners

Award winners were presented with their $50,000 Isaak Walton Killam Memorial Prizes at a special ceremony in Ottawa. These distinguished awards are given in recognition of outstanding achievements by Canadians in any of the disciplines in the natural sciences, health sciences, and engineering.

Stephan A. Cook, professor at the University of Toronto, is the winner of the Killam Prize for Engineering/Computer Sciences. He has made profound contributions to the development of computer science. In particular he originated the field of NP-completeness and helped to establish strong links between mathematical logic and the complexity of computations.

Stephan Hanessian, professor at the Université de Montréal, is the winner of the Killam Prize for Natural Sciences. He has made numerous contributions over a 35-year period to the study of organic chemistry, producing highly original and influential fundamental research. He is the premier international authority on carbohydrate chemistry and on chiron-based asymmetric synthesis. It is said that his approach to science has had a major impact on the way that organic chemistry is done today.

David H. MacLennan, professor in the Banting and Best Department of Medical Research at the University of Toronto, is the winner of the Killam Prize for the Health Sciences. He is a biochemist and biophysicist who has made fundamental contributions to the understanding of the mechanism of ion transport. He pioneered in work on the structure and function of the proteins of the sarcoplasmic reticulum, which regulate muscle contraction ion concentrations in muscle.

Appendix 7

The 1996 *Manning Awards*

The Manning Awards program was established to recognize and encourage innovation in Canada by honouring individuals who have created and promoted an outstanding new concept, process, or product that is beneficial to Canada and society.

Communications: Tim Collings of Burnaby, BC, developed the V-Chip, which permits parents to control the in-home television programming seen by their children. The inexpensive chip has been mandated to be built into television sets in much of the world. (Principal Award)

Industry: Tad Sudol of Edmonton designed, built, and licensed for worldwide use a portable system called the Sand-Vac for cleaning sand from the bores of horizontal oil wells. (Award of Distinction)

Survival: Vincent Thériault of Grande Anse, NB, designed an egg-shaped, totally enclosed lifeboat made from reinforced fibreglass. This innovative capsule protects passengers from rough seas, drenching, and hypothermia. (Innovation Award)

Cleaning: Bernie Graham of North Bay, ON, created the add-on VacPan for central-vacuum systems. It permits easy, hoseless cleanups from the kitchen and other smooth floors. Spilled material may be swept to a floor outlet, where a foot-operated lever activates the suction system. (Innovation Award)

Manning Young Canadian Innovation Awards

1996 Young Canadian Innovation Awards were presented to Haigo Djambazian, Montreal (bionic hand); Niladri Sarkar, Brossard, QC (cellular suicide sensor); Michael Richards, Wolfville, NS (algorithmic fingerprint image analysis and matching); and Dion Picco of Burin, NF, and Steven Lilly of Creston South, NF (three-dimensional toolkit for Windows 95/NT).